"Mike's story starts with the acute threat of death that I watched as a physician and his friend. As you read *Speak to the Mountain*, perhaps you may identify with the roller coaster of emotions, palpable struggles, and the uncertainty of tomorrow. For a season, the Palmers' future seemed to have burned up in ashes. Yet, once again, through the Lord's grace, He created breathtaking beauty from ashes."

— Stanley D. Yeatts II, MD

"Having had a front row seat for this amazing event so I can honestly say that nothing will ignite your faith like witnessing first-hand the power of God! And nothing will ignite your hunger like real life God stories. Mike Palmer's story will leave you Challenged, Inspired and truly knowing our God can move any mountain!"

— Ron Johnson, pastor and friend

"We all have valuable stories. Some can tell their story in a way that it causes life to spring up in our soul. This is one of those. Enjoy and you'll find yourself rejoicing through the tears."

— Dudley Hall, author of Grace Works

"Mike and Brenda came to us at Old Dominion University for a research project about aphasia treatment. God's timing was so evident as my assistant and I, both Christians, were inspired by Mike's tenacity in the face of great trials posed by the aphasia and the tremendous support provided by Brenda. By God's grace, Mike's aphasia recovery has surpassed expectations. To God be the glory!"

— Stacie Raymer, Professor of Communication Disorders,
Old Dominion University

"I've had the honor and privilege of being an eyewitness to the beginning of this story. I say the beginning because it's a long way from being finished. The story of Mike and Brenda's walk up the mountain will continue to reach and impact generations to come. It's been said that the big story of God helps us make sense of the littler stories in our lives. The Palmers' story helps us make sense of the gospel and our own stories at the same time. If you enjoy a story that makes you both laugh and cry, that both challenges and feeds your faith, you'll love *Speak to the Mountain*.

— Kenny Thacker, Founder of SoundWord, Inc.

"On the evening of May 24, 2000, Mike and I had a lengthy telephone conversation regarding bringing his newly designed vertical flow wind tunnel to market. Mike's design allowed one to experience the thrill of free-fall sky diving (without having to jump out of an airplane). I had recently retired from an aerospace company, where both Mike and I had worked, and I still had a number of contacts in the industry. A targeted potential customer was the Air Force and the training facilities at the Air Force Academy. We agreed to talk again the following evening to finalize plans for a trip to Colorado Springs.

"The next evening the phone rang. Assuming it was Mike, I answered. It was not Mike. It was his daughter, Amanda. She explained that Mike had had a massive stroke that day and his condition was dire, that he was in a coma and it was not known if he would survive. We never made that trip to the Air Force Academy, but Mike has, through the strong faith of him and his family, survived. Not only has he survived, but his design of his vertical flow wind tunnel has become the industry standard for amusement venues around the country."

— *Ray Knowis, VP Engineering (Retired)*
Micro Craft Inc.

"Mike and I both are engineers, love airplanes, and love the Lord. The story of Mike's fertile brain giving birth to 'SkyVenture' was reason enough for me to read this book. However, it is the rest of the story that describes Mike and Brenda's struggle to help Mike recover from his AVM stroke against overwhelming odds that riveted me as I read. I felt as though I was living with them and feeling their pain, uncertainty, and weariness. I was fascinated watching how they lived day to day exhibiting great faith in Jesus, and letting Him worry about how all this was going to turn out; how they depended on God's strength through prayer to get them through each day; the enduring love given to them by their family, friends, and church; and their unfailing courage to never give up, never give up on Mike's recovery! Best of all, the book describes how Mike and Brenda are using what they learned in their struggle to help fellow strugglers strengthen their faith in Jesus and move forward courageously into the unknown one day at a time. It is a story full of inspiration that everyone young and old should read."

— *Micky Blackwell, Executive VP (retired)*
Lockheed Martin Corporation

SPEAK
to the
MOUNTAIN

BRENDA PALMER
JENNY FIORE

UNITED WRITERS PRESS
ASHEVILLE, NC
2022

SPEAK *to the* MOUNTAIN
by Brenda Palmer and Jenny Fiore

ISBN: 978-1-952248-74-0

The photograph on pg. 52 courtesy of Sandy Torchon via Pexels.com. Cover photograph and all other interior photographs were provided by the author.

Published by:

United Writers Press
Asheville, NC 28803
www.UWPNew.com

To our grandchildren

Michael, Daniela, Sophia and Alex

so they will know the story of their grandparents and
find inspiration in times of hardship and unexpected difficulties
that they will, like all of us, face during their lives

Acknowledgment

I owe a debt of gratitude to Jenny Fiore for helping me bring the story of our family's journey to life.

I met Jenny when she was my daughter's neighbor. She was a young mom with two small children and I read her blog. Her writing was funny, creative and unique, just drawing you in. I knew she would add color and descriptions that would be so helpful in communicating our story.

Jenny was amazing throughout the process, always a good listener, and able to translate my thoughts and ideas into something that enhanced the story-telling aspect of the process. She is always gracious and I would totally love to do any kind of project with her in the future.

I highly recommend her to anyone who wants help in telling their story.

Brenda Palmer

"…for truly I say to you, if you have faith the size of a mustard seed, you will say to this mountain, 'Move from here to there,' and it will move; and nothing will be impossible for you."

— Matthew 17:20 NASB —

IT'S DEAFENING, THE SOUND OF your own body torpedoing through air. I don't know why people call it *jumping*. The word *diving* isn't right either. It's really a matter of *leaning*: You lean through the yawning hatch of an airplane and lie down on the air. The roaring wind catches you like a hammock and drowns out the pounding of your heart. A hair-raising ecstasy swells in your body, cell by cell, to the point of nearly bursting. The feeling isn't erotic, and it's too beautiful to be terrifying. Finally, an intense rapture and utter calm braid inside your body. The union makes surprising sense when you feel it, leaving scant room for fear. Belly-surfing on air, you take simple pleasure in the wind filling your mouth to a satisfying roundness. (Mine made an O. My cheeks rattled like maracas, and saliva curled around my lips.)

You don't worry about your chute opening, not like you thought you would. You've done everything right! You just savor this experience until you reach back and pull. What if nothing happens? What then? Will you wish you'd never flown?

Brenda Palmer never leapt from a plane, only experienced a simulated skydive in a wind tunnel engineered by her husband, but in all the ways that matter, she can tell you about the terror of a pull-cord that doesn't perform as expected. She knows now that expectations have a funny way of masquerading as faith. And I know, too, because she told me all about it, and now I'm going to tell you. This is her story of faith and expectation, and it all begins with a sandwich.

Jenny Fiore

1

Mike and Brenda on Alaska cruise shortly after SkyVenture opened in Orlando, July 1998

1

*And I will bring the blind by a way that they knew not; I will lead
them in paths that they have not known: I will make darkness light
before them, and crooked things straight. These things will I do unto
them, and not forsake them.*

— Isaiah 42:16 KJV —

Brenda was wiping down counters in her kitchen, aligning dish towels on their hooks as another minute rolled over on the oven clock. Her husband was poking his head into the fridge, and she knew he was homing in on those berries, one of his favorite foods. "Mike, don't eat the strawberries. They're for a recipe I'm making tomorrow night. Do you want me to make you a sandwich before you go?"

"Yes, thanks," he said. "I'll be in the office." Mike had an 11:30 a.m. tee time, and now he was flirting with being late. He was normally punctual, but he and Brenda had lingered in bed a little long that morning, enjoying the novel emptiness of their nest. They had taken their usual coffee and toast out on the patio instead of at the kitchen counter. Mike had read the newspaper, front to back. Then he'd gone to the grocery store to pick up a few things that Brenda forgot on her earlier trip that day. It was one of those deliciously lazy spring days, when the minutes ooze into hours, thick and sweet.

Brenda made a turkey sandwich the way her husband liked it. "Are you going to take this sandwich with you or eat it here?" He didn't answer, but she heard a muffled noise from another room, so she left the sandwich on the counter, rounded out of the kitchen, and walked up the short, dim hallway toward Mike's office, the corner room of their mid-century home, a delicious pocket of space with just enough room for the "man things." The thick and stout leather chair. The bookstack. The commanding wooden desk, half as big and twice as heavy as a Cadillac.

Brenda knew she'd find Mike on the other side of it, giving his usual serious consideration to one CAD file or another for his wind-tunnel project. Instead, she found him sitting, catatonic, behind his desk in his high-backed swivel chair. His head was tilted back, chin-up, with his mouth frozen slightly open. His eyes were blank. Her first thought was more of a wish—that he must be playing a joke—but hijinks were not Mike's style, and in her bones, she knew something was terribly wrong.

Patting Mike's cheeks and shaking him, Brenda yelled his name again and again. He showed no response, so she ran to the adjoining bathroom and grabbed a small towel from the cabinet. She cried out to God as she made a clumsy attempt at running the towel under the faucet, but she simply could not stay away from Mike long enough to soak it.

Brenda's hysteria was interrupted by the sound of the phone ringing. It made her swallow her screams long enough to try to speak. When she answered, nobody was on the line, but with the phone now in her hand, it dawned on her to call 9-1-1. She robotically touched the numbers on the keypad. The dispatcher that answered the call asked several time-stealing questions, which Brenda could barely comprehend in her frantic state. After answering enough of them, she finally got the words she wanted: "We're on our way."

How does anyone wait for an ambulance? There is no surer way to slow down the clock.

Brenda instinctively called her friend, Sandy, the pastor's wife at her church, a Pentecostal megachurch with a staggering headcount of nearly 2,500 members. In many churches, members believe—whether consciously or not—that the higher the clergy, the closer to God. Catholics have their cardinals, bishops, and Pope. Pentecostals have their elders, associate pastors, and head pastor. A hospital visit from one of the elders is the next best thing to one from the pastor's wife, which is right behind one from the pastor, who is the closest earthly connection to God.

That line of thinking was certainly the unspoken standard in their church, but it was never Brenda's way. She knew that goodness and strength were inborn in Sandy, not inherited or assigned. Even so, they lent no heavenly credits or superpowers, and friendship with Sandy transcended church politic and hierarchy.

"Hello? Brenda?"

It was unusual for Sandy to be home in the middle of a weekday. A megachurch never sleeps, and the pastor's wife is as busy as the First Lady, leading meetings and making appearances, doing community work, helping with services, and just being present for people in need in the congregation.

"Sandy, something's wrong with Mike."

Sandy heard the panic in Brenda's voice. "I'm on my way."

Though Brenda instantly felt less alone, she remained frantic, still trying to figure out what she could do for Mike. Time moved like molasses through cheesecloth. Impulsively, she reached out, grabbed his nose, and blew warm puffs of air into his mouth, trying to "revive" him though he was still breathing on his own. She felt warm air come out of his nose and onto her cheek—it wasn't doing him any good. She cried out loud to God again. Never, not even in childbirth, had she heard such animal sounds coming from her own mouth. It was as if someone else were screaming.

Unable to simply sit and wait, her mind wildly spinning, she decided Mike would be better off on the floor but how would she get him there? Brenda was a petite five-foot-four, and for the briefest moment, her animal fear morphed into anger. Here she was, neck-deep in terror, and her husband was just sitting there, unable to help. How could he *not* help her? This man had even pumped her gas for her; she had seldom so much as laid a finger on a gas cap in her life! Now he did nothing, and he was so heavy! These crazy thoughts left Brenda almost as quickly as they had arrived.

Putting her arms under Mike's armpits, Brenda tried to heave him up, but his body was limp and heavy as a sack of cement. He didn't budge. The impossibility of moving him made it seem that much more important that she get him onto the floor. Determined, she tried a second time, then a third. On her third attempt, the big swivel chair flew out from under Mike's legs, and she barely managed to guide his body as it crumpled to the floor. Now she could see the truth. Her husband didn't look like he was in shock or sleeping. He looked dead.

How many minutes had passed? Two? Thirty? Brenda resumed her irrational effort to perform CPR. This time, with each breath she blew, Mike's eyes slowly opened and shut. Again, she cried out loudly to God as she filled her own lungs for another breath and another and another and another. She knew Mike was not looking at her—or at anything else, for that matter—but the fact that his eyes kept opening told her he must still be alive.

Finally, the front door opened. Brenda heard footsteps quickly approaching the office where she knelt over Mike. It was Sandy.

The pastor's wife's face turned ashen at the sight of her friends.

"Oh, Brenda. Oh, Brenda. Did you call 9-1-1?" Sandy slumped against the wall and began praying out loud. Somewhere in the back of her mind, Brenda took note—this was the second person to pray for Mike since she had found him in this state. Power in numbers. Power in prayer. Now did God hear them?

Minutes later, the EMTs arrived, and right on their heels was a neighbor named Ben. Like Mike, Ben was a NASA guy, a contract monitor who had retired just a few years earlier. All tweed and loafers, large white teeth like tiles, and a rich-chocolate voice that carried for miles, he was a husky Virginia gentleman. He had big old Virginian composure and a beautiful accent unique to those parts. "Let's go *oat* to the water," he might say, or, "It's *aboat* time." Today, he was speechless.

Ben had seen the ambulance pulling up in front of the Palmers' home just as he was about to leave for a friend's 90th birthday celebration. Perhaps there was something he could do?

With local family roots that run five times as deep as they do wide, Ben also had a genteel but firmly masculine air that made him seem always in charge of the situation, like he owned the town. He was not the sort to panic, but even his stalwart air seemed shaken by what he saw after he hurried across the spring-green lawns between his home and the Palmers. Mike's lifeless body sprawled was a terrifying sight.

Ben clearly wanted to help but must have thought the situation looked hopeless. Was he watching a good man die? As with Sandy, his reflex was to pray. Ben cobbled together unhinged prayers, repetitive chants, the kinds one prays in a panic, pleas to an invisible father. He leaned against the wall with Sandy as he murmured them, watching from some distance without even meaning to distance himself. Here was a catastrophic situation lacking a person who knew what to do about it, a zeppelin careening toward the earth. What else to do *but* pray?

The EMTs struggled to get Mike out. They enlisted Ben's help in moving the giant wooden desk, which was blocking them from getting Mike on the stretcher. Ben looked relieved to be of practical use, and the massive desk felt almost light as it shifted with his help.

Yet the desk was only half the problem. The hallways of Brenda's and Mike's beautiful old home—narrow, dimly lit, and creaking with the moaning songs of old wood—instantly went from cozy and quaint to oppressive and tight, making passage of the stretcher next to impossible. And time was still passing.

Once Mike was loaded into the ambulance, Brenda was told to climb into the passenger seat. An EMT lent her a hand as she made her way up, her eyes firmly locked on the stretcher, looking for signs of life. Mike's eyes were fixed open and framed now by the metal of the stretcher and by the busy gadgetry of of an ambulance interior. One of the responders shined a light in his face and noted that one of Mike's pupils appeared to be larger than the other. Hands belonging to other medical personnel moved in and out of her line of vision, strapping things onto and around her husband. She couldn't shake the idea that Mike might already be gone.

That's when she noticed one of Mike's shoes peeking out from beneath the sheet, Blessedly, it moved.

Brenda glanced at the EMT at the wheel. "I don't know who you are," she said as the ambulance slowly pulled out of the driveway, "but one day, I'm going to find out."

The man nodded stoically, looking straight ahead as he drove. He was taking every precaution at each red light and intersection. Past the beautiful seagrass, beyond serpentine waters that snaked toward the coast, with a view of fishing boats pocking the distant horizons, the ambulance moved as if in slow motion. It drifted up the divided highway, slowing gently at turns, bothering with road signs and signals, using the proper lanes and never so much as lurching. Surely the sirens were blaring, but it seemed to Brenda that the thing was in no hurry at all. In fact, the normally 20-minute drive to the hospital seemed to take as long as it ever had in her own car.

Sandy lingered with Ben back at the house, the two of them unable to fathom what they could or should do in the wake of what had happened. Assurances were exchanged. He'd call the hospital later to check on things. She'd head over there on her own in the car. They locked the door behind them and parted ways.

Sandy's husband, Pastor Ron Johnson, met Brenda at Riverside Regional Medical Center, a major hospital sitting on 72 acres of the Virginia Peninsula. Ron was standing on the sidewalk at the emergency entrance as the ambulance pulled up to the roundabout. He immediately recognized that Brenda was too shocked to make even the most basic decisions, so he took over without discussion. She could barely breathe, let alone find insurance cards.

Brenda and Mike had had a somewhat peaceful and charmed life, so she hadn't really experienced true panic until now, but it coursed through her body as Ron walked her through the seemingly impossible act of just registering Mike through admissions. Then he asked her to give him the name of someone to contact in each state where she and Mike had ever lived.

In addition to their home state of Tennessee, they had lived in Florida, Alabama, Georgia, and Texas—the playing fields for major corporations in the aerospace industry, a trade that had kept food on their table for 20 years and counting. Brenda unearthed these names and numbers from a small notebook in her purse, handing them over with shaking hands. She felt frozen, numb, scattered, and deeply distracted. What was happening to Mike as she robotically signed forms and did as she was told? Where *was* he?

Finally, Brenda was brought to an examination room where Mike was stretched out on a gurney and hooked up to a ventilator. He barely looked alive. The room was sectioned off by a privacy curtain and, making it seem the sort of place set aside for extreme situations. Was this claustrophobia settling in? The room was the size of a small bedroom, its only provisions the gurney and sheets. She sensed that the size of the room was meant to provide an additional layer of isolation and privacy, which must mean it was reserved for the direst of cases.

Once Sandy arrived at the hospital, she joined Ron and Brenda in their holding pattern in the emergency room. Ron began the contagion of necessary calls to the contacts Brenda had provided to him. They, in turn, would make dozens more calls, eventually reaching out to a wide network of close friends from Fort Worth to Africa. While Ron made the calls, Sandy stood outside the examination room, praying. Theirs were the first bodies in a vigil that would grow exponentially over the coming hours. Word was spreading fast.

Watching the comings and goings of people in white coats and scrubs, Brenda noticed that nobody seemed particularly hurried. Nurses milled around desks. People pulled on drinks from water fountains, minding not to get their stethoscopes wet or let the wisps of their ponytails fall into the arcing stream. Soft-soled shoes squeaked and padded up and down the linoleum floors, bodies in casual motion casting shadows under the fluorescent lights. Were these emergency personnel?

Brenda felt alone in her urgency, in her desperation to quickly bring Mike back from wherever he had disappeared. Afraid to hope but afraid not to hope, she stood very still over him, staring at his salt-and-pepper hair, at the handsome face their daughter always said turned way too many women's heads. He was still wearing his golf clothes: a black and white shirt, black slacks, and an old pair of worn loafers. To her, he was the most beautiful man alive, and she was afraid she might be losing him. She put her hands on his hands and prayed.

IT IS AS MUCH CONFUSING as it is comforting to watch doctors and nurses go about their work when it's your own loved one stretched beneath their prodding hands. The man they worked on now came into Brenda's life in the fifth grade. In fact, she and Mike had been "a couple" since junior high.

Mike was widely respected among his peers as a brilliant engineer, the real deal, a *bona fide* rocket scientist. Nobody went lightly into a debate with Mike, who could make quick work of winning.

The project he had been working on that morning in his home office was nothing short of groundbreaking, the world's first aerodynamically designed recreational wind tunnel for simulated skydiving. In other words, Mike was walking virility, walking brilliance, walking confidence. But to these people slogging around him in white coats? Brenda sensed he was just another body on a table.

Mike's trademark as an aerospace engineer was an obvious intellect coupled with stoic humility. Though he was only in his mid-40s, his personality and profession had already taken him and his family through many cities and opportunities that thrust him up the career ladder doing wind-tunnel design and testing with big names like Pratt & Whitney, General Dynamics, and Lockheed. Such wind tunnels were designed to test and improve the aerodynamics and safety of planes.

Mike at Pratt & Whitney with experimental compressor for a jet engine

Mike at Lockheed looking over an experimental wind tunnel design

The recreational wind tunnel he had on his plate currently was an exciting twist on this longstanding work, a calculated career risk, an adventure of sorts for a man who was not one for taking risks in his business life. This project was commissioned work, brought to him by a zealously imaginative entrepreneur named Bill Kitchen.

Bill Kitchen's fortune was built on giving people a scream. He was a mogul in the recreation industry, a visionary behind innovative thrill ride ideas such as the popular SkyCoaster, which combines the sensations of bungee jumping and hang-gliding. When he dreamed up the idea of giving average Joes an improved way to simulate skydiving, he found Mike Palmer and believed that he was the man who could design the project.

Mike, excited by the idea of being a pioneer, was up to his elbows in this trailblazing project. Indeed, his prototype, the first SkyVenture wind tunnel, had opened a few months prior just outside Universal Studios in Orlando. Now the designer's brain and all it held—including critical engineering and operational thought—were under attack.

But what was attacking? This question taunted the doctors working to keep Mike alive. There was no official diagnosis yet, only theories. They knew he was

Orlando SkyVenture completed night photo

experiencing some sort of brain incident. Was it a stroke? If so, it was a severe one. That was their first theory. It was also the most convenient one, since the protocol for treating stroke is quite straightforward, and often the effects can be reversed if treatment is made soon enough. But if the doctors took that route and were wrong, the results could be catastrophic.

Some of the local people Ron had called were beginning to arrive at the hospital. Mike showed scant response to anyone, with the exception of the church's associate pastor, Don Rogers. Mike and Don were woodworking buddies, so they often spent a lot of their free time together. Brenda assumed this was why Mike moved his head ever so slightly toward Don when he heard Don's voice. The movement was barely discernible to others but, having watched Mike lay motionless for a while now, Brenda noticed even his slightest stirrings. Was he maybe awake inside there somewhere?

As Brenda waited, she asked one of the nurses to phone a family friend, Dr. Stan Yeatts, who was an OB/Gyn at Riverside Hospital. Stan was among Mike's closest friends, so it was not only because of his medical connection that Brenda wanted him nearby. This was an important call to make, and the nurse informed her it had already been made. Ron really did have things covered. Brenda, Sandy, and two other friends who had arrived at the hospital were taken away from the general emergency waiting area and escorted to a small, closet-like room away from the exam room to wait for news of Mike's condition.

When he'd gotten the voicemail message, Stan was nearing Washington, D.C., three hours into a trip with his wife Kim. This was all happening at a time before cell phone towers were ubiquitous, so reception was spotty. Able to make out only parts and pieces of the story, Stan and Kim prayed all the way to their destination. Once there, Stan called the hospital for news. That's when he realized the situation was more precarious than he suspected—Mike had been showing decerebrate posturing, a grave brain-damage "tell."

When a patient experiences decerebrate posturing, his body will stiffen as he hyper-extends his limbs, rotating his arms such that his elbows face away from his torso. He'll clench his jaw and tilt back his head. He'll bend his wrists forward, often as far as they can go. All of these postures are signs pointing to dramatic damage to the brain stem. Collectively, they imply that brain death could be just around the corner.

Stan, of course, understood the gravity of this report. Yet, with the heart of a healer and a strong faith in God, he also recognized that even terrible odds are not death sentences. They can be beat. Now he prayed that Mike's medical team shared that sentiment.

Stan wasted no time connecting with his peers on the hospital staff. Unafraid to intrude on behalf of a friend, he asked to speak with medical personnel working on Mike's case. Based on what information he could collect, and because of the uncertainty surrounding diagnosis, Stan noted it would be in Mike's best interest to be referred to an internist. However, a patient cannot be thrust upon an internist; the latter has right of refusal. Stan pressed and pressed, but no internist on duty that day would take Mike. The seriousness of his condition, Mike's precarious state, and the questions surrounding it, meant nobody wanted to accept the baton being passed on his case.

Finally, with Stan's persistence, Mike fell into the hands of a neurosurgeon named Dr. Jim Adam, who just happened to be nearby at his office that morning. Brenda was thankful a route had been chosen and was eager for answers. Her gratitude quickly gave way to anxiety once she met the neurosurgeon. His bedside manner left something to be desired.

Dr. Adam had blackish-brown eyes, walled off behind glasses, that sat in sharp contrast to his slightly graying hair and pink-fair skin. His mouth was a narrow line that pulled a little to one side of his wide, round face, as if in a smirk, except that he was very serious. He addressed Brenda with steely detachment and, it seemed to her, avoided meeting her eyes all the while. "Our CT scan of Mike's brain confirmed that he's experiencing a brain hemorrhage," he said. "It's substantial, but we can't know where that blood is coming from because there's too much fluid and blood in the way."

His words hit Brenda's ear like a radio broadcast, distant and canned. Her mental processes felt incredibly slow, so that she was grasping only bits of what was being said. Her mind chewed on these bits like gristle before realizing there was another word and another, spitting each one out to make room for the next, with very little chance to swallow any of it.

The words were tossed onto the scrap pile of evidence that kept mounting in the wrong direction—the separated room for extreme cases. The doctor who wouldn't look in her eyes. Was she really about to lose her husband?

"You have two options."

Dr. Adam said the word *options* with both gravity and detachment, the way they're said by someone offering rather than weighing said options. Weren't *options* the sort of things discussed on car lots, things like heated seats, all-wheel drive, and a moon roof? How could *options* apply to the fate of a human being?

"We can either perform surgery immediately to determine the nature of the bleed, or we can insert a drain in the area of the hemorrhage." Even as he spoke of cutting into her husband's brain, the doctor showed no hint of tenderness, no compassion, no sense of concern. In fact, there was no hint of any emotion at all.

"With the drain, we'll wait for the blood and fluid to sufficiently drain so that we can perform an arteriogram," he explained. "Then I'll be able to see exactly what we're dealing with."

Brenda continued listening without hearing. She'd have been hard-pressed to tie her own shoes in that moment, let alone process life-or-death questions. The words came at her like a shredded document, just fragments of sentences, pieces of words, tumbling into the air haphazardly. Brain and head and blood and fluid and tests. Brain and tests and fluid and head and blood. Their order didn't matter. They were all bad.

"If I go in and do surgery right now," Dr. Adam continued, "chances are I will do further damage to the brain because I can't see what I'm doing."

Zing. There it was. The phrase *damage to the brain* is what finally penetrated the protective space where Brenda's mind had been hiding for several hours now. It crawled into her ear and rang there, the only part of this robotic soliloquy that she truly heard. But not knowing what to do with the phrase, her mind refused to accept it. This doctor could not possibly be talking about Mike, she thought. Surely he meant someone else!

Ron and Sandy knew their role here. Though experiencing their own heartbreak over the situation at hand, they still had their wits about them and were behaving as if Mike were a family member, not just a friend and certainly not just another parishioner. With zero timidity, they asked the questions Brenda would have asked, had she not been in shock.

Perhaps the most important came from Sandy. "What would you do if this were your brother, Doctor?"

"You cannot ask me that question," Dr. Adam shot back. His eyes locked with Sandy's, and as they did, Brenda searched them for the slightest hint of compassion and found none.

For a moment, nobody spoke. Only the electricity running through the light bulbs could be heard.

Finally Brenda managed a question of her own. "When do I need to make the decision?"

"That's why I'm sitting in this room. You must make the decision right now."

2

*...And behold, the Lord passed by, and a great and strong wind tore
into the mountains and broke the rocks in pieces before the Lord, but the
Lord was not in the wind; and after the wind an earthquake, but the
Lord was not in the earthquake; and after the earthquake a fire, but the
Lord was not in the fire; and after the fire, a still small voice.*
— 1 Kings 19:11-12 KJV —

Raised by devout evangelical Baptist women and men in the hills of
rural east Tennessee, Brenda was raised to be a believer of the Bible
and parables. Her mother was the pianist at Oral Baptist Church, a surgical
nurse married to an industrial engineer, and the couple put church firmly at
the center of their family's life.

Left/Middle: Oral Baptist Church when Brenda was a little girl
Right: Brenda and her sisters dressed for Easter Sunday 1963

Brenda sometimes joked that she was probably birthed on one of
the church pews. She spent a good deal of her early life with her nose
buried between Bible pages and hymnal pages at Oral Baptist, her small,
strong body crawling under and between those pews as her mother played

accompaniment for the choir. The choir shook the walls as they practiced songs that would become the score to Brenda's childhood, songs like "Faith of Our Fathers," "My Faith Looks Up to Thee," "Great Is Thy Faithfulness," and "Trust and Obey." Songs about faith, faith, and more faith. These were sometimes joyful, sometimes solemn hymns, but almost always about letting God lead. They talked of the rewards of doing so and warned of the perils of taking any other tack.

Faith and obedience were of utmost importance in Brenda's family, with both of these so inextricably tied to love that it was difficult to distinguish them from each other. God was at the center of all things, a father figure in the pattern of Old South father figures—part tree-switch, part piggy-back ride, a mighty mountain that could both shake a room to its foundation and provide a place to curl up like a bug and stay forever small and safe.

Service to this mighty God in all things was the crux of daily life, with prayer mixed into the consistent refrain. Brenda, her two sisters, and her parents were often at the church, attending Sunday services both in the morning and the evening, and a prayer service every Wednesday night, not to mention the frequent choir rehearsals. Even on vacations, they dutifully went to worship. Then they brought home the church bulletins to prove it.

Oral Baptist was the picture-perfect image of a rural Tennessee church, a simple log structure with white clapboard siding. The church was located less than a mile from the three acres where they lived next to Brenda's grandfather's tobacco farm. Inside the church, there were places on the walls where the logs were rubbed smooth and shiny, worn down by the hands of many generations of small children looking for something to do during sermons that seemed to drag on and on. This was her mother's church, a place of patterned house dresses and fancy hats. White gloves holding marked-up leather Bibles with ribbon markers hanging out between their pages like dog tongues. Men sweating in good suits, some congregating outside before the service to finish their cigarettes and then coming inside to sing familiar hymns in low, country baritones. Children in black patent-leather shoes.

Brenda was just nine years old when she answered an altar call at one of the church's revival services. These altar calls were meant for people ready to accept Jesus as their savior. Brenda felt a strong pulling in her gut that day, telling her it was her time. The decision was the first step in a series of things she felt she had to check off to become a Christian. She didn't do it begrudgingly. On the contrary, going forward to that altar felt perfectly right and gave her a sense of peace that she was certain was not of her own making. The seed had long before been planted. Now she was ready to let it grow.

Without putting a great deal of thought into it, most of Brenda's decisions were made in one way or another from that seed. They were dictated, almost as naturally as taking a breath, a core of faith so deeply and passionately preached from the pulpit. And for decades after, she felt rewarded handsomely for her faithful approach to all things, as she was taught the faithful would be. It was part of an unspoken deal, one she didn't even realize she'd been making with God throughout her life: Trust in God, and He'll reward you.

Now, decades after answering that altar call, Brenda was discovering something uncomfortable and new about that unspoken deal. Here she prayed a continual prayer, and under the prayer, there was an itch, and the name of the itch was fear. What remained to be seen was whether it was a fear of losing Mike or a fear of losing God.

Like the parachute that doesn't open, perhaps God was not going to perform as expected. A husband lying lifeless on a hospital gurney was hardly an answered prayer, hardly a reward for faithful service, and the prognosis continued to look worse as the hours wore on. Thus began the real testing of Brenda's long-held beliefs, the real trying of her faith.

DR. ADAM'S WORDS HUNG IN the air: *You must make the decision now.* From a place of deeply held faith, how does one answer such a call? Empty her mind, open her heart, and wait for some truth to reveal itself? Listen closely for that "still, small voice" that parades as conscience but must be God? Brenda had been praying for hours already, and instead of even a moment's peace or clarity washing over her, the earth was continuing to open up and swallow her farther down. Now a doctor informing her, essentially, that she couldn't wait to do things in God's time. She had to make a choice in a surgeon's time, in medical time, or risk losing Mike.

At that moment, the door to the little room opened. Ron was standing there with his cell phone in hand, offering it to Brenda, telling her Stan was on the line. Brenda was overcome with relief when she put the earpiece to her ear and heard Stan's voice. She didn't waste a moment asking him for what she most needed in that moment.

"Stan, will you please talk to Dr. Adam?" she asked. "Will you make this decision for me?"

Without even knowing what decision was at hand, Stan immediately agreed. There was not a second of hesitation, and without saying another word, Brenda handed the cell phone off to Dr. Adam, who left the room with an air of relief.

Stan later recounted their brief conversation. "What would you do if this were your family member?" Stan asked Dr. Adam.

Coming from a colleague, the question could now be answered. "I'd do the drain and give it some time," Dr. Adam said decisively. Then he returned to the room to let Brenda know Stan's decision. A drain would be placed, and Mike would be moved to the ICU after the procedure was finished.

Someone reminded Brenda that she should phone her parents as well as Mike's to let them know what was happening. She recoiled at the idea, though she knew it was necessary. Dealing with her own confusion and pain was overwhelming enough on its own. She could barely stomach the thought of delivering heartbreaking news, especially without a diagnosis, prognosis, or hope. Her friends encouraged her to call them anyway, so she made both calls, telling them all she knew. She distantly heard them say they would get there as soon as possible.

Brenda then grabbed her things and set up camp in the ICU waiting area. The growing mob of friends continually stepping out of the elevator doors, one after another, would migrate with her. They followed Brenda now from the cramped space of the ER and into the larger waiting area that was about to become home.

PLACING A BRAIN-DRAIN WOULD REQUIRE minimally invasive surgery. Mike was already intubated, so step one was already done. He was wheeled into the operating room, then moved from the bed onto the operating table. A coma does not provide protection from pain, even in people who show no response to painful stimuli, which was the case with Mike when he was admitted to the hospital. It's more of a deep and mysterious sleep, a trapped existence, so Mike was given general anesthesia to prevent his brain from responding to pain signals.

Next, a small area toward the front and left of Mike's head was shaved, prepared, and framed in surgical drapes, a thin moisture-blocking material to help keep the area sterile. A local anesthetic was injected just under his skin at the surgical site, too—a sort of insurance policy to back up the general anesthesia and make certain Mike would feel no pain.

Surgery could now begin. Dr. Adam made a three-centimeter incision with a scalpel at the site, a slice about the length of an average adult's thumb tip. Then he removed a small section of the underlying membrane of connective tissue that protects the outside of the skull. A retractor was set in place to keep the area open for him as he worked. He used a surgical power tool to bore a small hole through the bone. Then he cauterized the protective membrane between the skull and the brain before inserting the small drain, a catheter that could now begin the work of uncovering the source of Mike's bleeding.

Right away, ruby-black cerebrospinal fluid began to flow into the drain. Normally, this fluid is colorless. The dark color confirmed the obvious, that Mike's brain had hemorrhaged. However, Dr. Adam saw no evidence that the bleeding was still active. Nor did he see any clotting. Finally, he tunneled the catheter under the skin and brought it out through a separate incision before removing the retractor. He sutured one layer of the opening, then sealed the next with steel staples before coiling the catheter several times and suturing it to Mike's scalp. The catheter was connected to a device that would monitor the fluid pressure in Mike's brain as the drain did its work. The waiting game was officially underway.

THE ICU WAITING ROOM WAS large and sterile, with couches, chairs, and tables situated in two U-shaped formations, dividing the room into two distinct parts. It was everything one might expect from a hospital last updated in the 1980s: muted pastels and brass and patterned linoleum. There was but one telephone, looking just as important and utilitarian as the payphone in a jail.

Located just outside the waiting room was the elevator. Each time its heavy, metal doors opened, which was often, a new familiar face emerged, arms open for a bear hug, launching into prayer. Brenda was grateful that not one negative word or inkling of fear was expressed to her.

One friend with a phobia of hospitals came to visit anyway and, when the elevator doors opened, he blurted to Brenda, "I have $35,000 in the bank. Do you need it?" Another friend pressed a wad of money into her hand as he came into the waiting area. But financial woes were not yet on Brenda's radar, so she didn't even consider accepting. Instead, she saw these offers for what they were: generous men desperate to give something more concrete than a prayer or words of encouragement. It was their way of giving themselves over to God as a tool, a means to give Brenda tangible proof that things were going to go her way. Each person who came off that elevator was doing essentially the same thing—offering themselves up as conduit for God's love.

More people were arriving than departing, so the room began to resemble a prayer meeting. Nobody wanted to go, because everyone, not the least of which was Brenda, was desperate to hear a diagnosis. They needed to know their prayers were working, prayers that meant the world to Brenda but had nonetheless failed to make the hands on the clock move any faster. In the middle of it all, agonizing over the mystery that loomed before her, Brenda had another enormous worry on her mind: telling her grown daughter and son the news.

3

Now we see things imperfectly, like puzzling reflections in a mirror,
but then we will see everything with perfect clarity. All that I know
now is partial and incomplete, but then I will know everything
completely, just as God now knows me completely.
— 1st Corinthians 13:12 NLT —

Even before Mike's incident, it was not unusual for Brenda to be in frequent communication with God. Forget about kneeling and folded hands. That wasn't the kind of praying she tended toward. Sometimes consciously and sometimes subconsciously, circling back to the scriptural father figure at the center of her life was as natural as breathing for her. She spoke to God between breaths, between sentences, as she moved from car to front door, from kitchen stove to dining room table, from everyday moments to the more profound. And though she felt heard and answered in some manner, she never fancied herself a medium. Brenda did, however, believe God sometimes spoke to one person through another.

Nine days before Mike's brain bleed, she had been praying about Mike in her car on the way home from a trip to the grocery store. The day was bright and blue, the impossibly tall conifers tangling with the equally tall deciduous trees in their late-spring splendor. Every bud was opened, every leaf matured. Poquoson, a wooded coastal beauty, is uncomplicated by buildings taller than two stories, its properties spaced at slapdash intervals, its main roads wider than necessary, its neighborhood streets narrow and shaded. It has a peaceful simplicity to it, in the traditions of old eastern towns that have endured the New World's test of time and have plenty more time yet to kill. Brenda found tranquility easy to come by here, whether on

21

her morning walks through the neighborhood or steering her car home from simple errands.

This day was slightly different, as had been the months behind it, because Mike's wind-tunnel project was at a pivotal moment: Though the prototype of his wind-tunnel design had fared well in Orlando, a bona fide tunnel sale was needed to keep things going. Mike's tunnel was new and unknown, a strange-looking oddity with scant history of operation and a hefty price tag, and Bill needed to start making a profit on it.

The risks of Mike having quit his job to take on this project were gnawing ever closer to the bone. He had bet everything on this tunnel, so a first sale was greatly needed. As with many prototype endeavors, the proof was in the public buying it. It was working as he had designed it, but was there a market for it?

On this day, Brenda was feeling a nagging sense that Mike needed buoying to help him along. There was an air of anxiety brewing in him. The line of his jaw looked tighter, his brow more knitted. The usual flash of energy in his eyes was flattening out, and he seemed almost uninspired, like a marathon runner at mile 20 in the race. This was an uncharacteristic response for an engineer to have in the face of a problem. Mike was normally energized by problems, viewing them as personal challenges to be conquered with a good dose of critical thinking, but selling the tunnel was Bill's job and not really in Mike's control.

As Brenda walked into the house that day with the last words of her prayer still falling through her thoughts, the phone rang. The caller ID showed it was a church friend named Lib. Brenda and Lib worked together in women's ministry, but they seldom spoke on the phone.

Mike, ever the workhorse, was almost always working at his desk during the day, so he normally answered the phone anyway. While Brenda unloaded the groceries, she waited for Mike to let her know she had a caller. Ten minutes passed without a word, so she walked down the little hallway to his office.

"Was that Lib on the phone?"

Mike was sitting at his desk, pen in hand, partway through scribbling what looked to be a very long letter on a yellow writing tablet. Brenda could see he had about five pages already written. He normally did his writing on a computer, so this longhand approach was unusual for him. He explained that he was writing out his thoughts in a letter to Bill. He was frustrated that a potential customer in California was saying that their "experts" had concluded that the steel structure of the tunnel was insufficient to meet earthquake standards. Mike knew that their opinions would add unreasonable costs to the tunnel, threatening the sale, and he strongly disagreed.

"She actually wanted to talk to me," Mike answered. "She said the Lord had instructed her to call me and to encourage me and to give me a scripture."

Now, this was odd. Mike didn't personally know Lib. Even stranger was the wild notion that God would reach out to a man like Mike in this manner. If God authored the personality type that would become an engineer, then God should know better how to communicate with one.

Who talks to a left-brained aerospace engineer using little voodoo-like messages on the tongue of a sweet little lady from church?

"What was the scripture?" Brenda asked. "Habakkuk 2:2-4."

Habakkuk is not exactly one of the better known books of the Bible. Mike had looked it up as soon as he got off the call. He now read it to Brenda:

> "And the Lord answered me, and said, 'Write the vision, and make it plain upon tablets, that he may run that readeth it. For the vision is yet for an appointed time, but at the end it shall speak, and not lie: though it tarry, wait for it; because it will surely come, it will not tarry.'"

Mike and Brenda had been attending so-called charismatic churches for a few years by this time. In fact, their current church had been caught up in a sort of spiritual craze spreading through similar churches around the country. Things like speaking in tongues and convulsing on the floor were making a regular appearance at their Sunday services, a change that left Mike and Brenda feeling somewhat alienated and uncomfortable. Brenda had become so skeptical of the goings-on that she even told God she couldn't understand why He would come up with such an idea as church.

Because of the shift, Mike and Brenda were growing increasingly accustomed to stories like Lib's. People in their congregation now received and relayed messages from God with some regularity. These were at least fascinating and far more palatable to Brenda than watching people writhing on the floor and choking on the strange language of tongues. She truly believed some of these messages were from God. The thing was, such stuff just did not happen to Mike. However approachable and easygoing he was, he simply was not the kind of guy to invite such a thing.

Yet Mike was so impressed with the scripture that, after later calling Lib back to thank her for it, he copied it into his daily journal. Naturally, he and Brenda were inclined to make the scripture fit some current happening in his life. This passage, so obscure and unexpected, surely was some instruction or assurance to Mike. Wouldn't it have do with the various challenges he was juggling with his wind-tunnel project? Mike personally wondered if the scripture referred to a previous journal entry in which he listed some specific personal prayer requests. And here, contrary to his usual habits, Mike was literally writing on a tablet at the moment of the phone call. "Make it plain on the tablets," it said.

Biblical scholars say the word *tablet* in this scripture refers to a foot-racing expression. In biblical times, during a race, a large tablet was held up to each runner at each lap, and on the tablet was inscribed the number of laps thus far finished. These tablets reminded runners of how far they had come as well as how far they still had to go. They documented endurance. They were tick marks, showing the passage of time during a difficult challenge.

Fast forward to the hospital where Brenda now sat awaiting news about Mike. Lib's call now made perfect sense. Just how many laps were still ahead of him? Brenda couldn't be sure, but she recognized that the next lap would be among the hardest: telling their kids the news.

Brenda felt it would be better to have some sort of concrete news to offer to the kids before making those dread calls. The mystery—the not knowing *why* Mike was in his condition—seemed too heavy a thing to set on their shoulders. Brenda preferred to carry it alone until the doctors gave her more to share. However, this wishful thinking soon gave way to the reality of the situation: answers might not be imminent, and doctors weren't giving her reason to feel optimistic.

Daughter Amanda was wrapping up her sophomore year of college five hours away at Virginia Tech. Brenda could not imagine Amanda driving alone in the car for five hours after hearing her father was in a precarious state in the ICU, so she turned to a friend named Joe for help.

Joe and his wife, Robin, were what Brenda and Mike called their "going-out friends." The couples had known each other for only a few years, but the friendship was easy and had quickly gained depth. They spent many hours together talking over lots of cups of coffee in restaurants around town. Mike got along like gangbusters with Joe, a home contractor and race-car driver. Robin was Brenda's sounding board and a favorite walking buddy.

To ask of Joe what Brenda needed to ask of him—that he make a 10-hour round trip to get Amanda—was at once enormous and not so enormous. It was that kind of friendship, and she knew that Joe meant it when, upon arriving to the hospital, he asked what he could do to help.

Just a week prior, Joe and Robin had attended their niece's graduation at Virginia Tech. Joe was scheduled to be in a race back home that evening, so his brother-in-law, who owned a private plane, had flown Joe back after the commencement. Joe immediately thought of that plane now. Could he maybe use it again?

Joe called his brother-in-law. In a blessed twist, the plane happened to be at the local airport, and the pilot was available. Joe dialed Amanda's number before take-off.

Amanda was participating in a special research project in advance of the summer semester at Virginia Tech. She was supposed to visit the lab periodically to jot down some measurements, but when she went to leave her apartment that day, her car wouldn't start. For weeks, the car had been acting up, but her dad had assured her when she called him days earlier that there was no need to worry. Now she was in a bind. She went back into her apartment, called her parents' house, and left an exasperated message before heading back out to try again. This time, the car started. She ran back into the apartment to call home again, but her phone was already ringing.

"Amanda, it's Joe. Can you do me a favor? I need you to pick me up at the Blacksburg Airport."

Since Joe and Robin were close family friends, the call didn't give Amanda cause for alarm. She assumed Joe must be flying in for one of his races, and she agreed to pick him up. On the way to the local airport, she stopped by campus and took down the measurements she needed at the lab.

The Blacksburg Regional Airport is as small as airports get. Amanda arrived there before Joe, and she killed her waiting time by looking at the posters and brochures inside the building. Many advertised flying lessons, an idea that intrigued her. As she sat calculating the costs and wondering how long it would take to get up to solo flying, Joe's plane landed.

When Joe walked inside the building, Amanda knew right away that something was not right. She could read it on Joe's face, in the sadness of his eyes and the way his mouth didn't even begin to curl up at the edges as he approached her. He didn't make her wait any longer.

"Honey, your dad passed out this morning and wasn't responding. He's in the hospital. You need to pack some things and come back with me."

At first, Amanda thought it was a joke, but even her own body wasn't playing along. She went instantly numb. Joe's unchanging expression, his eyes full of sympathy and pain, told her that the situation was extremely serious. Amanda's hands began to shake so hard, there was no way she could drive, so Joe took the keys and drove to her apartment so she could pack some clothes. They drove in near silence. She packed enough for only a few days.

There was no conversation on the plane trip back to Newport News. The loud, white noise of the engines meant everyone on board had to wear bulky headphones to protect their ears, but the roaring became a comforting sort of silence, syrup-thick with emotions that could not be carried on words.

When the plane landed in Newport News, Robin was waiting to take Amanda to the hospital. The pilot said goodbye to her in a most tender way, wishing her well. She was greeted in much the same way by the receptionist inside the airport. All of this fawning behavior would only add to Amanda's anxiety. Such careful treatment surely held some significance that meant her dad's situation was dire.

Stan and Brenda were waiting in front of the elevator doors when they opened to the ICU waiting room. Stan immediately began trying to explain to Amanda, with a doctor's expertise and a friend's sensitivity, what she was about to encounter when she saw her dad: *Your dad is not conscious. His head is bandaged. There is a drain coming out of it.* She could not absorb anything Stan was saying. The words ran through her like water through a sieve.

"Can I see him?" she asked.

When Amanda came to him, Mike was stretched out on the bed, unresponsive. The drain had been placed on the upper left side of his head, so a bandage was wrapped around his skull, making him look like a cliched Hollywood depiction of a soldier fresh from a battlefield.

Amanda leaned over him, her straight, tawny hair falling in a thick curtain alongside her cheeks. She wanted to hear him say, "Hi, Mandy." He was the only one who could call her that, the only one allowed to make her feel small and childlike. She touched his arm and talked to him, using a calming tone with words that would indicate nothing-doing.

Amanda spent the next several hours pacing the hallways, stopping now and again for a prayer or a hug with one of the many friends and family in the waiting room. Though raised on her mother's brand of faith, and deeply Christian herself, Amanda did not gravitate toward that sweet mob of congregational support the way that Brenda did. She was a "little Mike" in many ways, a code-cracking kind of analytical thinker that liked to learn. She would be the last to brag about it, but Amanda was often the smartest in the room and could logic her way through anything. She graduated a year early from high school with top grades in advanced classes, from orchestra to chemistry. Amanda's natural tendency was to look inward rather than outward to tap into God's strength. She was unafraid to seek spiritual guidance from elders and experts, but for raw hope and strength, she tended toward quiet introspection, deep thinking, and time alone to pray. To her, problems were for solving.

Brenda's and Mike's 21-year-old son, Stephen, was living in Dallas at this time. A gaming wizard, while Stephen was in his second year of college, he had been courted by a Texas video game development company offering him a dazzling salary for someone his age. The paycheck far surpassed anything he could expect to earn with a diploma right out of college.

He'd been with the company for two years now. It pained Brenda to think of the great distance and time Stephen would have to cover on his own between hearing the news and getting to Virginia. He still was skating that thin line between being a boy and being a man, living independently but with little life experience to draw on. Brenda could only imagine the agony of him being alone when getting the news and, perhaps worse, while making the trip to Virginia.

How could one bear to be alone with a sunken heart and the kinds of heavy unknowns that were at hand? She, at least, had the comfort of friends surrounding her in the hospital. Stephen would have no one.

One of Brenda's friends also had a son living in Dallas, David. David's mom was on the list of contact people Brenda had given to Ron upon arrival at the hospital. After Ron called her, the two of them agreed on a plan. She would call David, and David would deliver the news to Stephen. After he spoke with his mom, David called Stephen and asked to meet at a restaurant, where he delivered the news at the door. He then went with Stephen to help him get packed before seeing him off at the airport. Stephen was not alone in that dark hour after all. Brenda took this as answered prayer.

When Stephen arrived at the airport in Newport News, midnight was creeping up. He was greeted by Davis, a close family friend who had a heavy burden on his heart as he and Stephen approached each other at the airport, but Stephen had grown, was tall, and stood like a man who was prepared for anything that lay ahead. This boy was no longer a boy.

The two men exchanged very few words as they made their way to the hospital. Brenda would not remember the moment of Stephen's arrival. Nor would Stephen. The stress was simply too much.

ON THE MORNING PRIOR TO Mike's collapse, while doing some quiet introspection and prayer, Brenda had been reading the seventh chapter of Matthew in the Bible. In it, she came to a section about a man who brought his ill son to Jesus because his son was a "lunatic" that was often falling into the fire and water. The disciples had already tried unsuccessfully to cast out the demon in the boy, but Jesus took care of the problem with ease, casting out this so-called demon and restoring the son's good health and senses. The disciples were confounded: Why, they wondered, had Jesus succeeded where they failed? "Because of the littleness of your faith," Jesus said to them. "For truly I say to you, if you have faith as a mustard seed, you shall say to this mountain, 'Move from here to there,' and it shall move; and nothing shall be impossible to you."

Littleness of faith. This wasn't the first time Brenda had encountered this phrase in the Bible. She recalled it from other scriptures, wondering what it really meant. Why *did* that phrase appear again and again? Wanting to look at it in a more in-depth way later, she scribbled in the margin of her Bible: "Little faith?"

Now, in the late hours after most of the visitors were long gone from the ICU waiting room, Amanda finally stopped pacing the halls and sat down on a bench with Brenda. They slumped back together against a wall and exhaled. Fewer than twenty-four hours had passed since Mike fell into his comatose state in his office chair, but already it felt like an eternity. Mom and daughter were exhausted in a way they never knew possible. They sat together in the dimmed room without saying very much, each comforted by the presence of the other, both hurting beyond words and scared to voice their deepest fears.

Brenda wondered aloud how the plane trip with Joe had transpired. Amanda explained that not much was said—their conversation was a skimming sort of chat filled with the comfort of small, forgettable subjects meant to keep minds occupied, all of it buried under engine noise. Brenda looked at her daughter's small frame, at her thick, stick-straight mane of mousy brown hair framing her olive face and jay-blue eyes. Was she really only twenty? How could this grownup woman be only two decades old? Brenda couldn't see the resemblance other people saw, how very much Amanda looked like her at that age. This was perhaps because Amanda seemed so much stronger than Brenda remembered being. Amanda had always been a daddy's girl but a mighty one, the sort that could handle it all but quietly still needed her dad. After her first hour at the hospital, Amanda had shown remarkable stoicism and was able to provide a calming sense of comfort to her mom.

Frankly, she'd been collecting strength by leaning on friends in the ICU, but she wasn't hoarding it. She used what she needed and passed along the rest to Brenda.

"Was it a short flight?"

"Not bad."

"When did he let you know he was coming?"

"About two, I think. I was heading to the lab."

Soon they heard the clutter and squeak of a medicine cart rolling toward them. At the helm of the cart was an elderly black woman in a crisp, white hospital uniform. The woman noticed Amanda and Brenda and slowly steered her way to where they were sitting.

"Good evening," she said with a soft, crackly, old voice. "What brings you ladies here?"

Brenda and Amanda took turns telling her the events of the day. They told her of Mike's uncertain condition. They spilled it all. It felt cleansing to pour out this story together into a stranger, someone who wouldn't be pained by it.

After they finished, the old woman looked Brenda directly in the eyes with the most piercing intensity. It was intimate, like someone looking into her soul. "You do know what 'little faith' is, don't you?" the woman said. The question took Brenda's breath away. Her mind immediately flashed back to the scripture from the previous morning, and the note she had penciled into the margin. How did this woman know?

"No, I don't," Brenda answered.

"It means you need only a little bit of faith," the woman said. Then she turned and wheeled her cart away.

Brenda stared at the woman with an overwhelming sense of wonder. Then she told Amanda the significance of those words. The two of them took some measure of comfort in this unearthly encounter. Surely it meant God was near. They never saw that old woman again.

NOW THAT MIKE'S DRAIN WAS placed, his friends and family were doing time in limbo. The doctor would not do surgery until the drain ran clear instead of red. Long hours in the waiting room were punctuated by short visits in and out of Mike's room. To Brenda, it seemed as though the whole world had shrunk to this one floor of the hospital, to a starkly furnished waiting room and a tiny ICU cubicle.

Brenda, Amanda, and Stephen spent most of that first night huddled together in the waiting area. The minutes knitted together in long, slow loops that made the night feel interminable. Though she hated to admit it, Brenda knew she would not have strength for the marathon if she continued this sleepless vigil. At Amanda's urging, Brenda agreed to go home to shower and change, knowing Amanda and Stephen would make sure Mike was never alone.

Walking into the house gave Brenda a terrible, lonely feeling, as if she had stumbled into another time. Everything looked the same, which felt absurd. Her whole life was in flux while the house pretended otherwise. This home she loved so much, its cozy nooks and wide windows yawning around scenes of sky-tickling trees, now seemed lifeless and empty and cold. It held no comfort whatsoever.

Brenda shivered as she walked to the answering machine. Its red light was blinking. The first message was from Amanda the day prior, fussing at Mike for not being home to help her with some car problems.

"Where are you when I need you?" Amanda playfully asked before ending her message. The words stabbed at Brenda now. She sat back and listened to the remaining messages—dozens from people all over creation, expressing their prayers and cares for Mike—and felt great comfort but not nearly enough to anchor her down. She couldn't wait to get showered and changed and back to Mike's side, but she decided to email one impassioned plea for prayer to special friends who were thousands of miles away, missionaries in central Asia. She knew how fervently they would pray, but she only had the strength to type out the words, "Please pray. Mike has had a serious brain hemorrhage." Brenda knew they would be devastated by the news and the lack of details, but it was all she could give them.

4

Truly I say to you, whoever says to this mountain, 'Be taken up and cast into the sea,' and does not doubt in his heart, but believes that what he says is going to happen, it will be granted him.
— Mark 11:23 ESV —

By night two, the drain in Mike's brain was still not running clear. Watching the bloody fluid course through the tube became a waiting game that stretched on and on. Brenda, Amanda, and Stephen studied monitors, listened to alarms go off, learned the foreign environment of the ICU, and functioned in a daze. It was psychologically overwhelming for the family to leave and rest, but it was physically overwhelming not to.

They took turns. Stan and his wife, Kim, invited Stephen and Amanda to stay at their home that second night and at any time afterward when exhaustion hit. This meant the "kids" would not be coming home to an empty house, and Kim could make sure they were eating properly. It also meant Brenda spent the second night of Mike's hospitalization alone at home.

Brenda put off sleep as long as she could that night, not wanting to return to the lonesomeness of her empty house. As soon as she walked in the door, she made a beeline for Mike's office. Earlier in the day, someone had asked her if Mike held disability insurance. Brenda didn't know, but she was the mastermind behind the household filing system, so she knew exactly where to find all their insurance papers.

Attempting to read an insurance policy is difficult under normal circumstances. In Brenda's condition, the task was like working out mole equations while listening to free-form jazz and sinking into quicksand. With what little focus she could muster, Brenda managed to read enough to know that he probably had none.

She sat now at his desk, taking in the sight of the room and the chair where she had found him just a day earlier. His computer screen was brimming with icons for folders and documents and software programs that only Mike understood. These were mostly Greek to her. In that moment, fear gripped her so deeply, she couldn't quite remember how to breathe.

Brenda thought about calling Sandy for help but told herself to get up, turn off the light, and go upstairs to her bedroom first. She moved slowly, as if in a choking fog. She made it as far as the bathroom just shy of her bedroom before deciding she would try to get ready for bed before calling Sandy. She was still having trouble breathing, undoubtedly the effects of a panic attack, but the phone was right next to the bed, so she reasoned that she could hold off another minute or two. But once Brenda climbed into the bed, she instead turned out the light and cried out loudly to God.

"Please, Lord, put me to sleep!" The next thing she knew, the sun was trickling around the towering, skinny trees outside and shining in through her window. It was morning, and Brenda somehow felt rested. She immediately called the nurse to see how Mike was doing. Things were status quo.

Mike and Brenda's family was beginning to arrive from Tennessee after powering through a nine-hour drive. Brenda's parents and then three of Mike's sisters and two brothers-in-law drove straight to the hospital when they came into town. Mike's parents arrived separately by plane, wishing they had driven, what with a number of issues with booking flights and further delays. They each arrived at the hospital saddled with their own fears and pain. The sudden and untimely serious trauma of a loved one who is young and healthy is a jarring nightmare for any family. Because there is no warning or way to prepare, shock is inevitable.

In the overflowing ICU waiting room with so many gathered friends, Brenda found herself wanting to run away from the relatives. Their heavy pain and fear was accompanied by sadness and what appeared to be a lack of faith for a good outcome for Mike. She wanted to push them away, wishing they would leave and come back when this was over. She loved all of them but did not want them there. How confused and conflicted she felt by this unexpected reaction to such beloved people in her life.

Because of their long journey to get to Virginia, the family had not yet had the advantage of receiving bountiful encouragement, faith, and hope from friends who offered optimism and prayers for a complete recovery. They walked unprepared into a sterile hospital, filled to the gills with gathered mourners. They sensed death or severe brain damage on the horizon. Brenda did not welcome them with open arms. Their agony and disbelief was to be expected, but at that time, she did not possess the strength to endure it or even comprehend why she was reacting this way or to see it for what it was. To her, their presence brought added pain and heaviness, and she found herself needing to look away and distance herself from their grief, leaving her friends to comfort and receive them, which they did with great kindness and tender compassion.

Brenda found it easier to be honest with her own parents about her feelings, and when they asked her what she needed from them, she requested that they please leave the hospital, take care of things at home, and return occasionally to check on her. It was difficult for them to leave, but they did as she asked, returning occasionally for updates.

WHEN SOMEONE IS IN AN unresponsive state, visitors naturally harbor a quiet, magical hope that they will be the one to initiate some response. Some who saw Mike tried to get him to respond in their own way as they stood beside his bed. Perhaps they would see a foot move if they brushed against it? Would his eyelids twitch if they talked of the right subject, sat quietly enough, and looked closely enough? Would their voice or their touch do something?

The biggest encouragement in coma situations is to get the patient to squeeze someone's hand. Sometimes Mike did, and sometimes he didn't. The family didn't know if it was a reflex or an intentional response when he did. After all, babies have an automatic reflex that causes their hand to curl around anything placed in their palm. Maybe that's what Mike's body was doing, reverting to its most primitive state.

The neurosurgeon visited each morning to do a neurological assessment that looked rather sadistic to the family. Amanda seemed particularly hard-pressed to not snatch from the doctor's hands the pencil he used at these visits, laying the broad side of it perpendicular against Mike's nail bed. The doctor would press down as hard as he could, then squeeze Mike's trapezius muscle so violently, everyone else in the room would cringe. Judging from the fact that he slightly opened his eyes each time, Mike didn't like these things either. Blessedly, that meant he was conscious of them.

In neurology wards, these little brutalities are not only a necessary evil but also a standard one, part of something called the Glasgow Coma Scale. As the scale's name suggests, it's used to assess the relative consciousness of a patient suffering from a head injury. Three tests are involved in the scale: eye response, verbal response, and motor response. Each of these tests has a grading system. For example, there are four grades for the eye stimulus test: one point for no eye opening, two points for eye opening in response to pain, three points for eye opening in response to speech, and four points for spontaneous eye opening. Combining these tests, doctors tally points that add up to what's essentially a coma-severity score: A sum of three is the lowest and indicates deep coma or death. A fully awake person scores 15.

When Mike first arrived at the hospital, his score was a four. It had climbed to a seven by the end of his very first day of hospitalization. However, because the scale is not black and white and instead measures gradations in consciousness, it's no simple matter to name the moment when a person moves from being in a coma to not being in a coma. One can no more look at a flowering tree and decide when it is complete in its springtime bloom: There was simply a time when it wasn't in full bloom, and then there was a time when it was, and in the middle, there was a time when it was becoming. Mike was in the stages of becoming.

Once the family understood what the doctor was doing, they looked forward to his daily torture sessions. Even the smallest response from Mike could be translated into promise and hope. As visitors came and went, Brenda talked with Mike, held his hand, and tried to glimpse any sign of familiarity from his movements. Though the ICU had restrictive visiting hours in those days, Brenda and the kids were given uncommon access to Mike, apparently because the nursing staff sensed their need and seemed to recognize that their presence might buoy him. The family and many of the friends befriended the nurses and told them all about the comatose man now in their care. In their own way, they brought him to life, like Technicolor, showing off photographs of him and his interesting inventions, hanging these on the walls of his room.

Sandy brought a battery-operated tape recorder—the hospital had a strict rule against plugging anything into the walls—and the family played instrumental worship music. The nurses sometimes lingered for a bit to listen to the music, too. After a particularly rough day, when a woman in the adjoining room died of complications from stomach-stapling surgery, a respiratory specialist made a comment to Brenda that he sensed a lot of faith in Mike's room. Faith could be not only seen in the dozens of faces in the waiting room and at Mike's bedside but also felt.

Being part of an active church often means having a place on prayer chains. Sometimes you're the one doing the praying. Sometimes you're the one being prayed for. Sometimes you're both. More often than not, prayer chains are a many-tentacled thing extending well beyond one's own congregation. The names and pains of strangers are carried on the tongues of other strangers, uttered in prayer at mealtimes and bedtimes, in Bible studies and in quiet moments of time-killing contemplation at stop lights and in grocery store lines. More than one friend of an aunt of a friend was surely praying for Mike from day one of his hospitalization. People all over the world were holding him up in their prayers by the time the first day was done.

Among the strangers praying for Mike was a business owner named Kathie Schweickert, who lived and worked in Williamsburg, about a half hour from Poquoson. One of Brenda's friends had been at an appointment with Kathie and, knowing her to be a strong believer in prayer, asked Kathie to pray for Mike. At the time, Kathie was busy preparing for a trip she would be taking with her husband, Dave, but she promised to pray. She even clarified Mike's full name so she could be sure she was praying for him with specificity.

On Sunday morning, Dave and Kathie were enjoying the first full morning of their anniversary celebration aboard a Holland America cruise ship, cruising the western Caribbean, when they received a horrifying call. Their 21-year-old son, Spencer, had been shot in the head by a drive-by shooter while at a party and was in a precarious state in the ICU at Riverside Hospital. His sister, Tobi, was at the hospital with him.

As they frantically made plans to deboard at the next port, Kathie called everyone she knew, tapping into a prayer chain at every congregation she could think of calling. When she called her daughter for an update, she also asked her to find a way to contact the Bethel Temple prayer chain. It was the one Kathie had not succeeded in reaching yet.

"Mom, Bethel Temple is here at the hospital," her daughter said. "Somebody from their church is in the room right next to Spencer, and their people have been beside Spencer's bed praying for him, too!"

Stunned, Kathie remembered the prayer request she had received the previous day from her friend. Her son was now lying beside Mike Palmer, the stranger she'd been praying for.

ALMOST FROM THE TIME MIKE was hospitalized, Ron began telling Brenda that they were going to do as the scripture admonished them to do and "speak to the mountain." He repeated the message often and fervently.

"The Bible says we are to speak to the mountain, and that's just what we're going to do," he said. "We are going to ask the Lord to bring Mike back to 100 percent restoration. We will speak to this situation and say it will be removed into the sea." Whenever another friend or fellow church member arrived to the hospital, this same message was repeated. They passed it among themselves, like a mantra.

Ron instructed Brenda to be at Mike's bedside that Sunday morning for when he would call the church into prayer. Ron conducted two services every Sunday, so Brenda received two phone calls from him, one for each call to prayer that he led for the congregation. As Brenda held Mike's hand that Sunday, she knew she was standing in for the entire congregation.

Amanda attended one of the services with Ron's wife, Sandy, standing in the front row of the church like a daughter and a mother. Ron began the service by reminding the congregation about "speaking to the mountain," making an impassioned plea that they "pray corporately" for Mike.

Simply put, corporate prayer is group prayer. Many believe that this type of prayer follows patterns and purposes that are scripturally founded. The Bible teaches that whenever one or more of God's followers gather in prayer, God will be there. "Let us speak to the mountain of the blood clot and brain hemorrhage in Mike's head!" Ron commanded the church. "Speak to that mountain that it be removed and that Mike be restored to good health!"

The associate pastor, Don, joined Ron on stage, loudly instructing the church to pray for Mike's healing. Their entreaties were full of a sort of anti-venom, with Don referring to Mike's condition as an evil that had to be fought. He framed the ordeal as a battle of darkness and light, as if Satan himself were attempting to wrestle Mike from the hands of God. The two pastors spoke with their whole bodies, fist-pumping and pointing to the heavens, stamping their feet, and arching their backs as they spoke into their microphones with thunderous voices.

This was straight-up Pentecostal, get-on-your-knees, cry-it-from-your-heart kind of preaching, more dramatic than what the congregation was accustomed to seeing even in their deeply evangelical tradition. People in the pews began to flow into the aisles, many with their hands raised to the heavens as they cried out in prayer. Several gentlemen paced up and down the aisles, shaking with emotion, eyes closed as they leveled furious demands at God. It was as if everyone in the room were letting loose, and that's exactly what the pastors wanted. It was time to unleash every ounce of prayer power they had.

The steps near the podium began filling with dozens of people. One after another, they each took the microphone to intercede on Mike's behalf, passing it between them like runners in a relay. Amanda held her arm up, palm out, a position of both praise and entreaty. One of the deacons delivered Psalm 118:17: "You shall not die but live and declare the works of the Lord!" Another pastor predicted that Mike would someday stand on that very platform and declare with his own mouth the glory and awesomeness of God.

It was a service filled with exclamation marks, sweat, and tears. It could have melted metal off organ pipes.

Brenda was once told, "If you ever get sick, you want Pentecostals praying for you." As she listened now over the phone, she understood exactly why.

Still, by that same evening, the drain was not running clear, and Mike's condition was worsening. The fluid pressure around his brain had been rising and falling since the drain was first inserted, but now it was lingering at a dangerously high level. It was Memorial Day weekend, and Mike's doctor was out of town. Stan took it upon himself to meddle in the situation as much as possible, making sure the pressure numbers were brought to the attention of the doctor on call. It was decided that another drain should be inserted because the original one was malfunctioning.

When it was determined that Mike needed a second drain inserted, Stephen and Brenda were privately informed of the situation by the doctor on call. Having sensed the fears of Mike's parents and sisters, Brenda wanted to avoid the waiting area altogether until the procedure was done and asked Ron to be with them while she waited outside the ICU with Stephen. As the two of them sat together on a gurney in the hallway, Mike's dad came rushing to them in a state of great emotional anxiety. Brenda had never seen his dad so full of fear and panic, and she instinctively pushed him away without thinking, begging him to return to the family in the waiting area and pray. She was surprised by her reaction to him, but it was all she had left. It didn't take long for the insertion of the second drain. After the procedure, the doctor had some brutal words for Stan.

"Your friend will never be the same man he was before this thing happened to him." The words sounded like a quitter's curse where there should have been a healer's hope. Normally a gentle man—he's a favorite obstetrician among moms in Newport News—Stan laid into the doctor with the kind of anger that rises in defense of our deepest bonds with other people in life, the emotional bodyguard of those we cherish most. He left the doctor on call plainly aware that he was being watched and was not to rob this family of hope.

Nearly twenty-four hours after Kathie and Dave received the horrifying news that their son had been shot, their cruise ship finally reached its first port, Cozumel. It took them another twelve hours to complete the journey back to Virginia. It was Monday night by the time they arrived at his bedside. Brenda's heart ached for them as she watched their painful reunion.

As soon as they met, Brenda and Kathie had an immediate bond, an understanding of the agony and heartache of watching a loved one in a comatose state, uncertain of their odds. They had only to look into each other's eyes to understand. Neither had the strength to carry the other, but there was comfort in the unspoken sharing of their pain. Both were women of faith surrounded by people of faith. This blanket of faith provided some sense of security and calm, but it didn't change Mike's or Spencer's condition, so the families created additional ways to cope. Amanda walked. When she wasn't curled up in bed with her dad, talking to him, she walked the halls with Spencer's sister, who kept the nightly vigil with her. Their conversations were empty and deep all at once, each girl wrapped up in her own pain and aware that the other felt something similar.

Brenda and Kathie couldn't lean on each other, but they could dwell as neighbors in sorrow. It's often said that misery loves company, but the truth is that real misery is so lonely it leaves no room for company, just quiet communion. The two mothers looked at each other across the room sometimes as the hours passed, both in their own worlds of anguish, their eyes connecting now and again in a silent sharing of pain and sorrow. Occasionally one of them spoke of the pain she felt, tiny words to fill the quietness. Kathie showed an uncanny ability to transfer her burden over to God, and Brenda gained strength watching it.

When Spencer's four-year-old son arrived to the hospital, Brenda ached for him, remembering Stephen at that age. She thought of Stephen's suffering too, remembering the child within him as he came into the room now and again to sit near Mike. "Dad, it's Stephen," was all he could say. As only a mom can, Brenda knew the depth of her son's pain, however deeply he kept it hidden from others. While Amanda wanted to sit by Mike as much as possible, Stephen wanted to do the opposite, to get to the house and take care of things that could be taken care of—bills and insurance questions and anything else that might feel like progress. In and out of the room, Brenda's and Kathie's pastors and elders came. On opposite sides of the waiting area, their respective support groups gathered, sometimes crossing over into each other's side to add their prayers to one another's.

"What is this?" Brenda asked Kathie as people ebbed and flowed around them. "This is God in the flesh," Kathie said.

Brenda felt it was the perfect description for what she was experiencing, and the women sat quietly together again, waiting to see what exactly God was doing here.

AFTER THE SECOND DRAIN WAS placed, the pressure around Mike's brain began to stabilize, and the fluid in the drain changed from pink to clear. Now an arteriogram could be scheduled. Coincidentally, Spencer was taken for a similar procedure at the same time, which meant their room was left empty. Brenda found the sight eerie: empty spaces where two beds were previously parked.

An arteriogram is an imaging test that uses x-rays and dye to see inside arteries. Brenda was not allowed to accompany Mike to this test. She stayed behind and prayed. It was one of the longest hours of her life, but soon, if the doctors were right, they would know what had set the ball into terrible motion just a few days earlier. And they would know if it was fixable. When Mike's nurse returned from the imaging department to the ICU, she looked pained. Even though she was not authorized to give Brenda any information about the results, this nurse had grown quite attached to the family, and she wanted to prepare Brenda.

"Honey, I'm sorry," she said, "but they found an AVM." At the time, Brenda had no idea what an AVM was, but the nurse's expression spoke volumes. It wasn't good. Brenda felt the floor pulling out from underneath her, like quicksand. Her mind rushed to a possibility she had desperately tried to deny for three days: Mike could die.

The nurse left the room, and Brenda stood at the foot of Mike's bed, taking in the sight of him. She let her eyes scan over him from head to toe and back again. *What am I going to do if he dies?* she wondered. *How can I possibly let him die?*

She knew she had no control, and the possibility of being without him absolutely terrified her. Just at that moment, she felt a most curious tug-o-war taking shape deep inside her. It ached. What was this overwhelming sense that she needed to make a choice? Whatever it was, she felt it as deeply as she felt her love for Mike. As soon as she recognized the nature of this internal battle, she spoke her decision aloud.

"Yes, Lord," she said. "If you take him, I'm still going to serve you." Her declaration issued an instant surge of relief, as if her whole body knew in that moment that God was behind the battle, not trying to toy with her, not even trying to test her, but trying to reveal to her something crucial about her relationship with Him. She felt it was His way of showing her what was deep in her heart and, painful as it was, putting her love for Mike in its proper place. Mike had become something of a god to Brenda in their years together. Surely, this strange and sudden compulsion to blurt allegiance to God was about restoring correct perspective. Why else would it calm her as it did?

Brenda turned to leave the room, as utterly spent and exhausted as if she herself were on the brink of dying.

"Honey, are you okay?" the head ICU nurse asked as Brenda returned to the waiting area.

"No, I'm not."

Brenda had never admitted such a thing to anybody before in her life. The nurse quickly ushered Brenda into a small, unmarked meeting room and left her alone to collect her thoughts. Nobody else knew what had just taken place. A sense of isolation enveloped Brenda as she sat alone in this new knowledge that Mike might not survive. Not a soul knew what she had just said to God. She sat in stillness, astounded by it all. The thought of losing Mike was beyond her imagination, and then to decide she could go on living without and would continue to serve God even if He took Mike—these were things she never imagined she had the strength to do. She knew they were true now. She had crossed into a new level of faith. After a few minutes, Stan came into the room and learned what the nurse had said. He assured Brenda that she had been given the wrong impression, as he himself had been in the room when Mike's doctor read the rest results. The anomaly in Mike's brain was actually operable because of its position and size, and Dr. Adam would be in soon to explain it all in more detail. It was a whiplash moment, replacing utter despondency with true hope.

5

While other worldviews lead us to sit in the midst of life's joys,
foreseeing the coming sorrows, Christianity empowers its people to sit
in the midst of this world's sorrows, tasting the coming joy.

— Tim Keller —
Walking with God through Pain and Suffering

In medical imaging, it looks like a child's scribble or the tide-twirled tentacles of a tiny octopus. But an AVM, or arteriovenous malformation, is a snarl of malformed blood vessels in the brain. It can present as a single tangle or as many clusters in the brain's circulatory web. This rare congenital defect can go undetected for years or even a lifetime. Though AVM ruptures are generally less deadly than most types of strokes, Mike's situation was grave. At this point, all that could be said was that the AVM had not killed him, but he certainly wasn't out of the woods. He would face surgery, and the outcome was still unknown.

Dr. Adam, the neurosurgeon who initially seemed so detached, came into the room looking almost perky. Could this really be the same sourpuss that Brenda first met at the hospital? Perhaps in his position, he too often saw grave situations that ended catastrophically. Maybe he was concerned that without his steely demeanor during the early stages, he'd give false hope to families.

Grabbing a pen and a napkin from the table, Dr. Adam began diagramming the procedure he would perform on Mike's brain. If Brenda could have mustered the energy to smile, she might have: Over her decades with Mike, she had watched him sketch hundreds of ideas on hundreds of napkins. She knew he would have gotten a kick out of watching the doctor sketch what he was about to do to Mike's brain.

45

Dr. Adam explained that surgery would begin with shaving Mike's entire head, not just the surgical site. It was hard for Brenda to imagine Mike without his turf-thick hair, black as a moonless night, with one striking circle of silver-gray in the front. Such a loss was no loss at all now. Dr. Adam explained he didn't want Mike's hair growing out in a strange way. "That man has the nicest head of hair I've ever seen in my life!" he explained.

Surgery was scheduled for mid-day on a Thursday, exactly seven days after Mike's arrival at the hospital. Dr. Adam said he expected it to last for three hours. In simplest terms, he explained how the whole procedure would play out. He would begin by clipping the blood supply to the problem, and then he would remove the clotted AVM. The size of the AVM was relatively favorable, but its location in the left hemisphere of Mike's brain was cause for some concern because the doctor couldn't be sure how Mike's speech might be affected.

Brenda mentally swept aside this bit of information, partly because she'd never been around anyone with a speech impairment. At this point, she was concerned about Mike's odds of survival—they appeared to be good—and about any physical handicaps that might linger. Speech problems didn't seem like much of a handicap in the grand scheme now, not when Mike's entire right side appeared to be completely out of service.

Mike was showing vague signs of consciousness, but it was uncertain which were mere reflexes. Sometimes he seemed to furrow his brow at the sound of a familiar voice, for example. His hand might curl around an object placed in his palm. There were no profound ah-ha moments that left anyone with clear indication he was cognizant or that the real him still lingered somewhere within that trapped brain.

The time that followed Dr. Adam's visit was filled with prayer, conversation, quiet moments of reflection—your basic treading of water. Mike's condition was upgraded to stable, and everyone was in a holding pattern. Friends continued to come and go with regularity. Brenda spent nights at home, with Amanda holding overnight vigil. She could not have gone home if Amanda weren't keeping watch, and when Brenda did leave, all she could think about was returning. It was a familiar feeling, like she'd had about her babies when they were young.

THE TENNESSEE WINTER WAS BLEAK and heavy in 1978 when Mike flew into Florida for his job interview with the respected aerospace firm Pratt and Whitney. Rushing to get to the Knoxville airport for his morning departure, he failed to latch the front door to their rented house on his way out. Brenda, tired and round with child, woke to find Old Man Winter had crept right into their bedroom. She certainly didn't need any persuading from Mike when he called to say he wanted the job in Florida. The place sounded wonderful. He told her that as soon as he got off the plane in West Palm Beach, it was all a done deal in his mind.

Brenda and Mike put the down payment on their first home, a humble and boxy little thing in Jupiter, Florida, a town of about 7,000 people on the south end of the state. Mike had just graduated, so the house was a basic Florida starter home: a three-bedroom, one-and-a-half-bath with a carport that sometimes doubled as extra space for woodworking projects. The front door was painted a predictably garish Floridian turquoise, and the bathrooms were decorated with Pepto-pink tile. The price tag was a meager $34,000. That was the absolute most they could afford, even as Mike was accepting a well-paying job. (He had also received offers from Lockheed and McDonnell Douglas, but neither of those big dogs could offer him the Florida sun.)

The Jupiter house might not have been a beauty, but the life that Mike and Brenda would build there over the next two years had a pleasant simplicity to it that spoke to their young, Tennessee-mountain hearts. While Mike's job certainly had its pressures, the quiet town of Jupiter that contained it had a slow and lazy feel to it, like a sun-drunk vacation that never ended. The couple's yard was sandy and filled with citrus trees bearing grapefruit, key lime, oranges, and lemons. Brenda and Mike could pluck the fruit right off the branches for a juicy treat on a hot summer day.

They turned the back room of their house into a workshop, where Mike's radial-arm saw could be heard buzzing on many a weekend afternoon. In the early years, after Stephen was born, Brenda would sometimes walk out and find him toddling around in the sawdust.

Mike with one-year-old Stephen in Florida

For fun, Mike and Brenda took little Stephen on bike rides and for outings to the beach within a mile of their house. Sometimes they ventured to Blowing Rocks, a farther beach where there were natural cut-outs and tunnels in the rocks leading to the surface, made by the passage of time. As the waves crashed against the rocks, water blew up through the holes, and Stephen would wait eagerly between each eruption, welcoming them with unfettered glee.

Sometimes the family drove to Palm Beach to see how the other side lived, steering their humble Volkswagen Beetle around the bodacious curves of mansion-stuffed neighborhoods. It was a high life beyond anything they'd ever seen. Their own "high life" amounted to the occasional dinner at the Burt Reynolds Dinner theater, not far from their home. They even celebrated their anniversary there in 1980, when Brenda was two weeks past due with Amanda.

Mike and Brenda easily made friends at their new church home in Florida, the First Baptist Church in nearby Tequesta. That was no wonder. Both were talkers, social creatures who loved nothing so much as good conversation about meaningful, interesting things such as engineering, God, and babies. If such topics weren't already on the table, the couple could always be trusted to put them there. Their conversations ran the gamut from intellectual to spiritual to all the silly and curious spaces in between. With their new friends, they swapped parenting stories and whiled away many long, lazy days, well after the Florida sun went down.

These were their first married-life friends, connections that would run deep and shape the couple's ideas about friendship itself well into the future. Indeed, it was in this earliest part of their marriage that they recognized the importance of a church community in which to couch their social lives. Church was where great friendships were made, but it wasn't just shared faith that deepened these first friendships. It was the larger shared experiences, the time in life when the kids are young and when marriage is new, everyone getting the hang of the grownup thing. The wives swapped babysitting and recipes. The husbands set up tee times. Their firstborns became big brothers and sisters. Separate families became like extended families, and people who had so recently been mere teenagers, grew up together.

This was a time of learning—for Brenda, how to be a mother, and for Mike, how to have a serious job and support a family. Mike was happy at work, which was beneficial in more ways than one: sometimes when he came home from the office, Brenda couldn't hand over the kids fast enough. Exhausted, she'd hightail it to Kmart just to get a chance to exhale.

The funny thing was, no sooner was she down the road at that store than she'd start missing the very same little people that had just made her so weary. It was the typical mother's paradox, that the majority of a badly needed break would be spent pining for the creatures that created the need for said break.

Two DECADES AFTER THOSE LAZY days in Jupiter, Brenda felt those old feelings being resurrected. Her body, mind, and spirit desperately needed breaks from Mike's bedside, but she spent those breaks agonizing about being away from him. In fact, the breaks were more of a chore than anything. She raced through them, sleeping only as much as necessary, showering in haste, ignoring the ever-expanding pile of mail, and letting the Tupperware salads and foil-wrapped casseroles pile up in the freezer and fridge to precarious heights. Even making a quick run to the hospital cafeteria was hard for her. As much as she knew she needed breaks, as soon as she got them, Brenda couldn't wait to return to Mike's side.

Brenda could force herself to leave Mike's side from time to time only because she knew that Amanda would take over the sentinel duties in her absence. Mike was never alone, day or night. When Amanda wasn't with her daddy—that's what she called him, even at her age—she was pacing the halls or recharging with sleep at Stan and Kim's house.

One evening, Brenda came into Mike's hospital room and found that, while Mike was not alone, Amanda was not the one holding vigil at his bedside. This was odd. Nor was Stephen or even a family friend standing at the bedside. Instead, it was Spencer's dad, Dave. He was praying for Mike, a breathtaking generosity of spirit that deeply moved Brenda to her core. This experience circled back to a major theme Brenda had experienced for decades, that faithful Christians naturally form bonds with each other.

But things were declining for Spencer as things were looking up for Mike, and the reality of that situation weighed on everyone. Kathie and Brenda saw less and less of each other, their loved ones' trajectories traveling in opposite directions. One morning when Brenda arrived at the hospital, Amanda met Brenda in the ward wearing a stricken look on her face. She explained that Spencer had suffered a stroke during the night, and Kathie had just been informed. Brenda went to Kathie immediately and, in a rare moment, found her alone. There was no pause or awkward moment of not knowing what to say or do. Brenda just put her arms around her without even thinking, one mother to another. She found herself saying a version of the comforting thing she herself was continuously being told: "Lord, please give Kathie what she needs right now."

The hospital staff separated Mike and Spencer that day, and Spencer died soon after. By the time Brenda heard the news, his parents and all the people who had come to pray for this beautiful young man had left the hospital and gone home. There was a new emptiness in the ICU waiting room now, and it stung, a painful reminder to Brenda of a truly incredible loss.

6

I am certain that I never did grow in grace one-half so much anywhere
as I have upon the bed of pain.
— Charles Spurgeon —

The ICU is not a place where people want to be alone. It's full of unfamiliar sights and sounds, machines that beep and screens aglow with cryptic information. Each new beep is startling. Changes in the patterns of lines on the screen or the cadence of machine noises are just as worrying. Tubes and connections and medicines traveling from bags hanging on poles offer a disturbing view.

Brenda had many moments when she was alone with Mike in the ICU. She stood at his bedside, holding his hand. As she spoke, she searched his body and now-stubbly face for any signs of waking, response, or just being himself. She told him again and again where he was and continually reassured him that he was being cared for by a wonderful team of doctors and nurses.

Brenda preferred having the nurses in Mike's room with her. It was such an isolating experience to be standing by her husband's bedside, looking over his body, and yet somehow not really have him with her. The nurses made her feel less alone. Yes, there was the constant flow of prayerful friends out in the waiting area, but that was where Brenda preferred most of them stay so she could protect Mike's dignity: he was diapered, intubated, bandaged, and literally slack-jawed. Yes, her children came and went from the room, and even Mike's parents and siblings rotated in and out of the room. Perhaps the difference with the nurses was that they were caregivers not only to Mike but also to Brenda. As they tended to Mike's physical health, they seemed like earthly manifestations of the hands and feet of God, tending to Brenda's spirit.

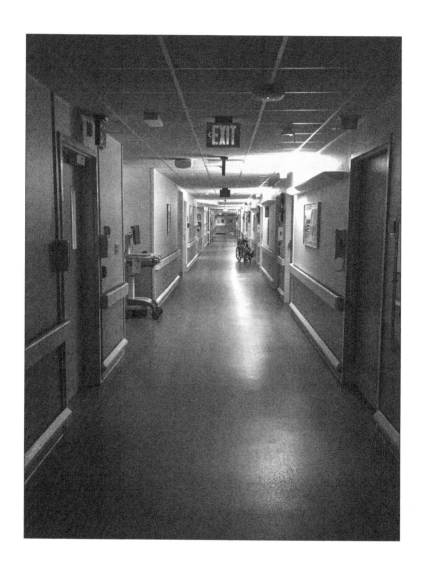

When not providing some sort of care to Mike, the nurses took turns perching on a chair at the foot of his bed, working away on charts about him. Their job, of course, was to keep him alive, and as Brenda watched them, she felt certain they were exceptionally good at doing that sort of thing. She sometimes stopped to admire the way they engaged with Amanda and Stephen, always taking the time to chat, explain changes, and make sure the kids were comfortable. They did the same for Brenda, perhaps even more so. In fact, she felt like they were advocating for her as much as for Mike.

Knowing Mike was in such good care made it a little less difficult for Brenda to peel herself away from his bedside from time to time. She *needed* those breaks. She *needed* to spend time with friends and family in the waiting area. She *needed* their presence as a body needs water.

The morning was so bright the day Mike's surgery was to take place, and the summer sun pranced in flickers on the surface of the water of the tributaries winding around Poquoson.

Brush-bristle seagrass bent gently in the breeze, and it struck Brenda as incredibly strange that most of the men and women driving the wide roads to their jobs at NASA and the shipyards had not a clue about the enormity of the day ahead. Mike Palmer was about to have brain surgery!

When she arrived at the hospital, she kissed Mike on the cheek, squeezed his hand, rubbed her fingers along the hairs of his arm. Brenda had no way of knowing what—if anything—Mike knew about the day ahead of him. Much had been said in his presence. Much had been explained to him. It didn't matter that he couldn't respond. The family needed to keep believing he was simply trapped somewhere in the deepest center of his own mind, hearing but unable to make his body to show it.

As Mike's bed was rolled out of the ICU enroute to surgery, its wheels made a creaking sound on the old linoleum. Someone pulled the thin white sheets up high on his body, covering him the way little children cover themselves with their blankets when they're scared of the dark, all the way up to the chin. At the touch of a button, the extra-wide doors to the surgical area slowly opened, and Mike and the nurses were swallowed up into the ominous room and bright light beyond. Brenda felt like a caged animal. She decided to get out of the ICU waiting area while the surgery took place, choosing instead to sit with two friends in the main hospital lobby. The high-ceilinged room was peppered with big potted plants, their spiky green leaves providing the vaguest sense of privacy between chairs and loveseats upholstered in modern, geometric patterns. Brightly lit with sunshine pouring in through the bank of windows at the hospital's entrance, the area felt a little less suffocating to Brenda. And sitting with good friends helped distract her.

Amanda and Stephen were also in the waiting area, but they kept separate vigil with other friends and family. Each of them found their own ways to draw strength, knowing they had not enough to give to each other. Some families might sit in a tight circle in such situations, leaning quietly on one another, holding hands, curling up in the crooks of each other's arms. That simply was not how this family coped. Instead of shrinking inward, they turned to their extended family, their friends. They sought strength from those who had reserves of it, who could replenish them. They opened up their own little family circle to include dozens of others, and it made them feel stronger.

The surgery was expected to take three hours. As she waited, Brenda sometimes prayed but talked very little. In her mind, she was reflecting on and took refuge in the simple words a friend had said to her that morning.

"Today you are going to have many opportunities to choose life or death," he said. "Go toward life each time." She resolved to do just that, not knowing how but willing herself to believe she'd figure it out. Stan promised to let Brenda know as soon as Mike was out of surgery, and she found herself thirsting toward the elevator doors every so often, far before the surgery could possibly be done. Dr. Adam accurately predicted how long the whole thing would take: three hours after surgery started, Stan came off the elevators and brought Brenda news that the surgery was a success. By that, he meant only that Mike had not died on the operating table.

Mike was later brought out of the recovery room and transferred back to the ICU, heavily sedated and unresponsive. His head was covered with a white turban-like bandage, and though she couldn't see it, Brenda knew that he was completely bald. He looked a bit of a fright, his skin still a not-right hue, the breathing tube coming out of his drawn mouth and tethering him to a ventilator. Dr. Adam explained that, despite all appearances, Mike was no longer considered to be in any kind of coma and would most likely wake up very slowly.

After several hours, as he slowly came out of the deep spell of anesthesia, Mike's eyelids began to flutter just a little. Then, for the first time since Brenda had found him catatonic in his office, he was able to really open his eyes. She could see again their bright green irises, which now had no hint of a twinkle, just the flat look of shark eyes. Mike gazed up toward the top of his head and then at the ceiling, where he continued to hold his stare for some time. Brenda and the kids said a few words, letting him know they were there in the room with him, telling him they loved him.

In the hours that followed, Brenda and the kids stood by Mike's bed, talking to him whenever he seemed to be awake. They doted, fussed with the sheets, and placed his hand in theirs, ran their fingers softly against his cheek, appreciating the warmth of his skin. It meant life. They repeated again a simple version of what had happened to him—how he had collapsed in his office and then had a blood clot surgically removed from his head—so that he would know where he was and that they were all there with him. The nurses encouraged them to keep repeating the information, because they weren't likely to recognize when he could hear them, and he wasn't likely to retain what they were saying as he continually moved in and out of sleep.

"Mike, this is Brenda."

"You're in the hospital."

"You have something wrong with some blood vessels in your brain."

"Stephen and Amanda are here."

"We love you."

"You are going to be fine."

Eventually, Mike began turning his head and following simple instructions to squeeze the nurse's hand, always using his left side because the right side of his body still was not moving.

Each time Mike's vitals were taken, the nurses also checked to see if he would respond to stimulation of his feet. They ran a blunt instrument up the lateral sole and across the pad under his toes. A person with healthy brain function will respond to this "plantar stimulation" by curling his toes downward. A person with a central brain problem will respond by curling one or more toes up, indicating that the signal running down the spinal cord is not quite normal.

Eventually, Mike's toes curled down. The nurses put external intermittent-compression devices on the lower half of Mike's legs to lessen the chance of blood clots forming. These reticulated, air-filled tubes looked like giant swim floaties, cartoonish in their bright blue color and proportions. They made a large, rhythmic whooshing sound as they repeatedly inflated and deflated. The nurses also placed ankle-supported shoes on Mike's feet because of his extended prone position and the fact that he was not moving his right leg or foot at all. The shoes looked like clunky orthopedic moon boots, crazy old-man gear, cinched across the tops of Mike's feet with wide Velcro tabs that made a loud noise when being repositioned.

Brenda tried her best to anticipate Mike's every possible need and keep him comfortable. She also shaved his face each day. Mike obviously didn't care how he looked, but it mattered to Brenda. She wasn't sure if the urge was fueled by a desire to comfort herself, protect his dignity, or make sure the medical staff saw him as a person of worth. Mostly, Brenda was just fighting for anything that would make their impossible situation seem more normal.

A new stint of agonizingly slow waiting was underway, and none of the family voiced aloud what they were all painfully wondering: How much did Mike actually understand? Would he ever speak again? And worst of all, did he even recognize who they were?

Between his visits to the hospital, Stephen continued to take care of things at his parents' home, making sure bills were being opened and sorted. The piles were growing tall. Amanda continued her approach of talking with her dad in her usual unflappable tone, as if nothing particularly strange was afoot. She never gave him any indication of the true depth of her distress, hopeful that the whole, real, perfectly intact him was only temporarily trapped behind that dull faraway look in his eyes.

"Hi, Dad," she would say. "You look pretty crazy in that turban, you know."

After two days of this painful waiting, of feeling utterly unsure that Mike even heard a word, even knew who she was, Brenda finally took a break and went to the mall. She wanted to get some pajamas for him, even though Mike never wore pajamas at home. It was just that his sick and weakened appearance in a hospital gown had become unacceptable to her. Though he wasn't moving on his own, he could be made to move so that she could dress him. Yes, new pajamas would be just the thing.

Of course, Mike didn't even know what he was wearing, let alone care about it, which only made Brenda redouble her efforts to add some glimmer of normalcy to their situation. These small acts of reminding herself and others that Mike was so much more than a patient in a bed, gave her little pieces of strength. She was taking the broken fragments of the man she knew and repositioning them to create a new order, like turning a kaleidoscope to make the pieces fall into a new arrangement that makes its own kind of sense.

As she walked through the aisles of the men's department, Brenda found herself growing increasingly frustrated. She suddenly wanted to scream at the other people in the store. Why were they leisurely shopping for clothes? The idea that anybody could be doing such a trivial thing while her husband lay paralyzed in a hospital was sickening, too much to bear. She was in and out of the store much faster than she intended, pajamas in hand, feeling like she might come out of her skin if she saw one more smiling shopper swinging heavy bags of who-even-cares-what.

The next day, Mike finally moved on his own. It was just a small, reflexive movement, but he was definitely doing it on his own. The movement began in his toes and was followed by the slightest shifts in his legs—*both* legs. There was still no movement in his right arm or hand, so the nurse instructed Brenda to keep massaging that hand vigorously.

"Draw as much attention to it as possible," the nurse told her. "Just keep at it."

Brenda did as instructed, but Mike ignored the hand altogether. Even as more and more movement returned throughout the rest of his body in the coming hours, he continually reached for things with his left arm in awkward, inefficient movements. Then, almost imperceptibly at first, he began lifting his right leg at the knee. His right side wasn't paralyzed after all!

Twelve days after he was admitted to the hospital, Mike was finally ready to be taken off the ventilator. It was June 6. The respiratory specialist asked Brenda to leave the room while he divorced the machine from Mike's body. Extubating—removing the breathing tube from the throat of the patient—is not something especially suited for an audience. Typically, the patient does a fair amount of coughing and hacking. Rarely, if the patient struggles to breathe on his own, immediate re-intubation must take place, a process uncomfortable for the patient. It's difficult for the uninitiated to watch.

Waiting outside the room, Brenda allowed herself to hope Mike would speak once the tube of the ventilator was out of his throat. Hearing his voice would mean the world to her. When she returned to the room, however, that hope was dashed. Mike was able to breathe fine on his own without the ventilator, but he didn't utter a single word, nor so much as a sound. She encouraged him to speak, asking him how he was feeling. He didn't seem to even try to reply. Instead, he continued to silently stare at Brenda, following her movements with his eyes and obeying only the simplest of commands. She smiled at him as if all were well, but she was crushed.

7

My days have passed, my plans are shattered. Yet the desires of my heart
turn night into day; in the face of the darkness, light is near.
— Job 17:11-12 NIV —

Cell phone use was strictly prohibited on the ICU floor, so most calls came
through the landline of the squat, beige phone in the hospital waiting
area. Several of Brenda's friends took turns manning the thing, because she
simply didn't have the energy to continue giving reports on Mike's condition.
Out-of-state calls were the exception, especially those from Bill Kitchen.
The SkyVenture wind-tunnel project was in its critical stages of development,
and Brenda knew Bill was anxious about what was happening with Mike's
progress. She wanted to be the one to speak to him when he called. It didn't
take many conversations before Bill decided he was coming for a visit. Brenda
knew it was inevitable, and she braced herself.

Enroute to Virginia, Bill stopped to pick up an ex-girlfriend, perhaps
feeling she would lend him moral support. Brenda and Mike knew the
girlfriend from their time in Orlando, where the tunnel prototype was built.
They regarded her as a good friend, and she had already called to check on
Mike at the hospital from time to time before Bill asked her to accompany
him. Brenda suspected Bill was nervous to come alone, uncertain what he
was going to encounter when he got to the hospital.

Bill arrived during the morning hours. Brenda did her best to prepare
him for what he was going to see, but she could tell he was uneasy. Rather
than go into the ICU to see Mike right way, Bill offered to treat Brenda
and the kids to lunch as his first order of business. During lunch, he talked
nonstop and effusively of his desire for Mike to come back to work with him

on developing the wind tunnel, and he assured Brenda that he would help in any way he could.

Unsure of the recovery road that stretched out ahead of Mike, Brenda didn't know what to say. She stuck to polite and general conversation.

When they returned to the hospital, Bill wanted to take his laptop into Mike's room.

Laptops were new technology at the time, and he thought Mike would be interested, that he'd surely show some reaction. Brenda knew in that moment just how ill-prepared Bill really was for the truth. She led him into the room, where Mike was blankly staring as usual. Mike hardly reacted to Bill, much less to the laptop, and not at all to the pictures Bill showed him of his newly acquired Russian jet. In fact, it was unclear to Brenda whether Mike even knew who Bill was. He just blinked at him. Bill opened the laptop and put Mike's hands on the keyboard, but Mike did not move them in response. Slowly, slowly, he just shifted his gaze downward to look at his hands resting on that sea of numbers and letters that Brenda wasn't even sure he recognized. He had no reaction, as if his hands had been propped on a pillow perhaps or not moved at all. She wasn't sure he even recognized them as his own.

Discovering Mike in this state surely left Bill reeling. On top of the pure shock of seeing this broken man, Bill had to be wondering how on earth the SkyVenture project would move forward. He said nothing of it, of course, and Brenda didn't ask. She also refused to follow that line of thinking too far. First, the idea of Mike not being well enough to continue the project— ever—scared her. Second, falling prey to that fear went against everything she was taught about the nature of God. The Bible claims that "God heals all your diseases." Brenda felt that if she believed the Bible, she had no choice but to believe that promise. The alternative was to learn to live forever with the devastating effects of a catastrophic brain injury. Bill left without discussion of the precariousness and uncertainty of Mike's condition.

After two and a half weeks of recovery, Mike was deemed ready to move out of the ICU. His next stop was a surgical "step-down," which is pretty much what it sounds like: a recovery area that is one step down in intensity from ICU. Brenda, Stephen, and Amanda were told they couldn't visit Mike until he was settled into his new digs. It was late afternoon, and though they didn't have much appetite among the lot of them, they left to grab a bite to eat. They needed something, anything, to help them kill their waiting time.

As they drove, and over dinner, it registered with Brenda that her kids were transforming before her eyes into much older versions of their former selves, taking on responsibilities far heavier than anything they had ever faced. She now thought about how God calls all people *brothers* and *sisters* in biblical scripture, encouraging us to not neglect one another. Having her kids together in this crisis, she felt connected to them in ways she never had before.

By the time they returned to the hospital, the stars and moon were on full display in the Virginia sky. They stopped by the ICU waiting area to retrieve their belongings. The large room was empty of people, and even the lights were turned out. The waiting area had never been emptied during the entire time of Mike's stay, and Brenda felt as if they were players in a theater production that was now finished, stage lights dimmed, props and scenery moved to a new set in a new theater. Leaving this space felt almost eerie. Her final thoughts were of Spencer.

"Let's go find Dad," Amanda said.

The spacious step-down room was staffed with 24-hour nursing care and had four beds, each separated from the next by curtains and outfitted with basic hospital-room furnishings, including a ceiling-mounted TV. When Brenda and the kids walked into the room, they found Mike situated in the first bed to their right. The head nurse greeted them with a big smile and gave them a quick run-through of their surroundings and the new rules of play.

"There will be at least one or two nurses in the room at all times," she said. "Even though you won't be allowed to stay overnight here, one of you can be with him throughout the days." The thought of Mike being unattended by family all night was troubling for Brenda.

Amanda had been staying overnight all this time. Now, just like that, her days of wandering the hallways and sleeping on sofas and vacant hospital beds were done, and Mike was going to be entirely in the hands of strangers for hours on end.

Brenda and the kids stayed with Mike as long as they possibly could that evening. They made smallish talk around him, trying to keep things light and act naturally to put Mike at ease, just in case he wasn't. Nobody could be sure. When it was time to go, Brenda felt as she used to feel when the kids were little and had to be left with babysitters, not sad so much as compassionate, hoping Mike understood but knowing the only way he probably could was for the process to happen and be repeated until it was routine.

The days afterward slowly piled into a week, and as visitors came to see him, Mike sometimes made the subtlest nod or tilt of his head or an ever-so-slight widening of his eyes, but he gave no hint of a smile. He wasn't even close to showing true expressions. Everyone wanted to hope, but nobody could say for sure how cognizant he really was or ever would be. All continued to speak to him in encouraging words, as if everything were fine. Then, finally, Brenda received her sign.

There are certain familiar ways that long-standing couples hold hands. Just as they lay claim to a particular side of the bed and cling to it for a lifetime, many hold hands in a particular way that becomes mindless habit, muscle memory for the whole of their relationship. One day, as Brenda reached out to grab Mike's hand, he repositioned it so that he was holding it the way he normally did on their walks. He cupped his hand over the back of hers, curling his fingers through the openings between hers, like a fist within a fist. This tiny gesture held real significance to Brenda. It was a sign of Mike being Mike.

Now that Mike was conscious, therapists checked on his condition every day, some more often than others. In particular, the respiratory therapists, speech therapist, and physical therapist began coming in and out of his room with regularity. With their help, Brenda tried to focus on what Mike *could* do. She and the kids took some measure of joy from a significant milestone the day after he was extubated: He ate!

For the most part, Mike was still being fed intravenously, of course, because choking was a huge concern at this stage of recovery. But, by God, he managed some food on his own. Pretty much any food that could be pulverized could be attempted. Unfortunately for Mike, even things like steak could be pulverized—and were.

The next order of business was to help Mike regain some control over the movement of his body. With brain injury, it's typically unclear how much progress will be made during rehabilitation, both in the short-term and during the patient's remaining life. You try, you hope, and you move forward without deadlines. Change can come in a day, a month, a year, decades—in the body's own time. It could be compared to watching water come to a boil, except in the case of brain rehab, there's no guarantee the water will ever boil. It is an exercise in hope and patience. And it is a journey across new territory, like relocating to an unfamiliar place and having to start all over again, something Mike and Brenda had experienced in spades.

Top: House in Georgia
Bottom Left: Family in Georgia; Bottom Right: Mike in a low-speed wind tunnel at Lockheed

8

It was when I was happiest that I longed most...
The sweetest thing in all my life has been the longing...
to find the place where all the beauty came from.
— C.S. Lewis —

In the late 70s, during their two years in Florida, Mike was periodically wooed by Lockheed in Marietta, Georgia. Another aerospace giant, Lockheed was the company for which he had worked as a co-op student while in college.

Lockheed management preferred to hire the company's co-op students because of the time and money invested in training them. Not only that, but Mike was damn good at his job. He was deemed a quality investment, so the company continued reaching out to him with ever-increasing salary offers, even after he accepted the Florida job. Finally, the numbers got big enough and the opportunity enticing enough—work in advanced aerodynamics — that Mike and Brenda decided it was time to bite. This was in the fall of 1980.

The day their last box was packed and the little Florida house was empty, the Palmers said their goodbyes and braced for a new adventure. Amanda was six months old. Stephen was two and a half, an age when a child's orbit grows large and begins to overtake whole rooms and then an entire house. He was no longer content to be plopped down in a corner with a heap of blocks and books. House-hunting would be a whole new ballgame this time.

The housing market in Georgia was in a slump, with properties being sold on the cheap. Armed with a sweeter salary, Mike and Brenda were able to purchase a significantly larger and nicer home than the one they owned in Florida. It was a cedar-sided, modern-looking, three-bedroom tri-level in

West Cobb County in a quiet suburb of Atlanta, about twenty minutes from Lockheed and all the major shopping areas. The house had a garage on it like a great big yawn, a perfect open space for Mike's woodworking projects, which filled his weekends. The whole place felt big and modern and spacious to Brenda, almost cavernous when they first set up their things.

The size and multiple levels of the house, combined with Stephen's age, resulted in a sort of circus of daily calisthenics for Brenda. The theme song from *Benny Hill* would have made great background music. For the first few years, she was always moving a child-safety gate from level to level to level.

As the kids grew older and the safety gates came down, Stephen and Amanda began to explore the outdoors, spending their days playing in the spacious yard, which backed up to a farm. Warm summers fell on the heels of comfortably cool springs, and the sunshine was as ample as it had been in Florida, if less warm. Sometimes, late-day showers took the edge off the hotter summer days, and the kids would run in from the rain, laughing and dirty and wet-headed. In the fall, the trees turned into kaleidoscopes before dropping their colors to the ground where Mike raked them into giant confetti piles. The kids leaped into them feet-first, dove into them face-first, and laughed themselves silly.

Brenda and Mike loved it here, but they both felt a longing for something more. They wanted "a place," which was code for having land to call their own. They kept on the lookout for the just-right property, and around their fourth year in Marietta, they found it.

Buying five raw acres of land was terribly exciting for them. The piece was nicely wooded land but also rocky, so much so that Brenda was convinced a vein from nearby Stone Mountain ran through it. There were no buildings on the property, so they could make of it what they wished. On evenings and weekends, they loaded up their old green Volkswagen bus and drove the five miles from their house to their land to do the work of building a structure where they could live. The plan was to build a good-enough place that would keep them warm and dry and comfortable while they built a larger home. The first building would then become Mike's woodworking shop.

Except for pouring the foundation, they didn't contract out a lick of the construction, opting instead to do everything with their own hands. Mike was crew chief, farming out jobs with the efficiency of, well, an engineer. The kids were asked to pitch in wherever possible, and not just as a gesture to make them feel a part of it all. No, they really were *expected* to help, and they did, whether it was carrying a bucket of rocks or sanding wood.

City codes required that the structure be a minimum of 1,300 square feet. Mike designed the space so that, on the first floor, there was a bedroom with a walk-in closet, a bathroom/ laundry room, and a central room used for a kitchen/living area. Above the bedroom, he partitioned off a loft space that became Amanda and Stephen's bedroom and play space. Within the year, they were able to move out of their old home and into the new building on their own land.

The whole family thrived in the new place. The location was beautiful, and it was all theirs, five wooded acres to explore. The kids trudged off in the mornings after their bellies were filled on breakfast, little explorers with big imaginations. Sometimes they burned up nearly all the daylight hours, building forts and living just as dangerously as they pleased. Together, they kept the harmless, wild secrets of young children set free, climbing where they shouldn't, poking at nests and crevasses, going barefoot on rough ground. If they fought, Brenda wasn't likely to hear about it. She made no secret of her low tolerance for bickering and didn't mince words when she told them they had to get along or else. It was clear to the kids that any problems they had with one another were best worked out without Brenda having to take a hand in the peacemaking.

"You two *will* get along," she commanded if they started to fall apart at the seams. "This isn't a choice. It's not a suggestion. It's a rule." Brenda and Mike found joy here, too, not only in their cozy home and with their dreams of the "big house" on the horizon. It wasn't just the mild winters and the lush springtimes, not the crisp autumn days that let the warm summers rest for a spell. It was, again, a place where they found good friends, other young parents with unfolding dreams of their own. As was the case in Florida, many of their friendships were formed at church.

During their search for a church, Brenda met a woman named Bernadette, "Bernie" for short, who also had two kids at the time. She was married to Dean, an optometrist who was just starting a private practice.

Their families' lives were running at a sort of parallel, and they quickly formed a deep friendship. Brenda and Bernie spent lots of time together, shopping for sales, discussing parenting strategies and going to yard sales where they bought more than they should, filling their closets with toys for the kids' Christmases and birthdays. They swapped babysitting with each other to make time for the couples to have their own date nights, too.

Bernie and Brenda often took the kids to Sun Valley Beach in the summers. It wasn't a real beach. It was a man-made one on thirty-three acres in the woods. Trucked-in sand surrounded a massive amoeba-shaped pool that could hold a whopping 1.5 million gallons of water, the largest pool in the Southeast. On one side, there were a series of giant, colorful slides snaking into the water. The centerpiece of the whole monstrous delight: side-by-side kiddie slides with a fake mama dolphin whose baby was perched atop her back. The mama's spine was curved as if she were leaping out of the sea. The original brochure for Sun Valley Beach read, "You don't have to leave town to go to the beach." Mobs took heed. The summer crowds were big, and parking was hard to come by. Families came in flocks, picnic blankets in tow, slathered in cheap sunscreen and hauling beach bags filled with toys and books and munchies. Bernie and Brenda and the kids dragged straight lines in the sand with their dime-store flip-flops as they trudged toward a good spot, not too close to the snack bar but not too far from its bathrooms, lest some child needed to go "number two" or make the highly unlikely choice *not* to pee in the pool.

Bernie was a Tupperware dealer, and Brenda was one of her best customers. Between them, they boasted one of the most organized picnics on the beach. The critical piece was a giant orange-and-white-striped Tupperware carrier. Bernie and Brenda took turns packing it full of sandwiches and other snacks for the kids, who came running and screaming and wet from the water to take ravenous mouthfuls before running back for more swimming.

Eventually, as the kids got a little older, they grew tired of Sun Valley Beach. Though a fixture of their summer days, it felt stale. Each curve of the slides was as predictable as the last, the splash into the water at the end nothing more than an anticlimactic been there, done that. By the time Amanda was in the first grade and Stephen in the third, the group outings were switched to

Six Flags White Water instead. The families bought season passes, and again, hauled their orange Tupperware container full of sandwiches. Sometimes their husbands joined them, but Dean was busy building his practice, and Mike often needed the daytime hours to sleep, because sometimes he needed to work the night shift at Lockheed.

In Florida, at Pratt & Whitney, Mike had worked within a group that built jet engines. He was involved in design as well as overseeing fabrication of one-of-a-kind jet-engine parts. It had been a nine-to-five job handling what people in the aerospace business would consider exotic materials—extraordinarily expensive stuff that requires high tolerance to costly testing using jet fuel, also not cheap. A million-dollar project was but a drop in the bucket, when a compressor component, for example, could cost an easy five million, so one of the first things Mike noticed at his new job in Georgia was that Lockheed was not nearly so loose with its project money. With the kind of work he was doing there, they didn't have to be.

Mike was part of the Advanced Aerodynamics Department, an intellectual breeding ground for new concepts and new modifications for existing aircraft. The job had him deeply enmeshed in the science of flight. The primary lab used for this type of work is a wind tunnel, which is essentially a structure that simulates the effects of air on objects. Scientific wind tunnels have been part of the aircraft industry from the dawn of human flight, starting with the Wright brothers at the turn of the 19th century. (The automobile industry also uses wind tunnels to test aerodynamic performance and conduct noise-level research, but wind tunnels are used primarily to measure forces on aircraft.) Unlike with jet-engine testing, tweaks and changes were not a big deal and could be managed within a matter of minutes or hours, as opposed to months. This real-time quality of wind-tunnel testing gave Mike a sense of more immediate reward and steady momentum. It was an excellent fit.

The tests he conducted usually took place in the evenings. He would be assigned to a project, work on the math and details, and then take the model or project he created to the wind tunnel for the testing phase. These tests lasted for several weeks, and then the process would begin again. It made for a slightly clunky schedule on the home front, but Brenda and Mike made the best of it. He was, after all, enjoying his new work.

Mike worked on wing design and wind-tunnel testing for what was called the "C-X" program, a concept eventually awarded to McDonnell Douglas that would become the widely recognizable C-17, a prized cargo craft of the military. He also did various wind-tunnel tests for concepts of the C-130, components for the widely used Advanced Warning and Control Systems, wing design for the world's largest transport aircraft (the C-5 Galaxy), and various other projects.

This job laid some of the critical groundwork for the recreational wind tunnel Mike would end up designing just before his brain bleed. But during his time at Lockheed, *recreational* wind tunnels weren't really a thing at all. The only tunnels of this type in existence were outdoor devices called aerodiums and an indoor facility called Flyaway, which used the same technology as the aerodium.

Aerodiums are constructed with an airplane propeller in the bottom, separated from the flying area by a screen. Would-be fliers stand on the screen, lean into the forced air from below, and attempt to steady themselves atop it. The air velocity is not high enough to keep them afloat in their street clothes, so they have to sport baggy flight suits. While the suits add enough drag to keep the flier buoyant for a spell, staying steady is quite difficult, and the fliers easily fall off the air column, landing on cushions that surround it. This "ride" is more of a brush with flying than a replication of skydiving, with the flier spending most of the time attempting to stay on the air. Mike's design, on the other hand, would hold the promise of changing not only skydiving simulation for the general public but also for training of airborne military troops. In a world where it seems like everything's been done, he created something truly groundbreaking.

9

*Try to exclude the possibility of suffering which the order of nature and
the existence of free wills involve, and you find
that you have excluded life itself.*

— C. S. Lewis —

Recovery from a catastrophic brain injury could be compared with reassembling a once-finished, thousand-piece puzzle that's been dropped on the floor. There might be whole areas of the puzzle found intact, but others are a chaos of shapes in disarray. There are so many places you could start to rebuild those shattered sections, some coming together more quickly than expected, others leaving you hunting way longer than you'd like. If there are pieces missing, you won't find out until you've worked hard on putting together the rest. It still wasn't clear to Brenda, Amanda, or Stephen if Mike knew who they were, though they dared not voice their fear to each other. The way Brenda saw it, putting Mike back together was entirely in God's hands. She prayed that God would make Mike whole again. If she trusted, she felt He surely would, but not on her deadlines or anyone else's.

She regarded the team of people who were working daily with Mike as hand-tools of a divine creator. Among that team were respiratory therapists. One or another of them dropped by each day to gauge his progress and administer treatments, usually with something called an *incentive spirometer*. This is a plastic graduated cylinder out of which extends a short, reticulated hose with a soft mouthpiece. Inside the cylinder is a rubbery plunger. The plunger would rise from the bottom as Mike blew into the mouthpiece. The more air he could push out of his lungs, and the more forcefully he did so, the higher the plunger went. It was like a respiratory version of the familiar "high striker," or Strongman's game, played at carnivals, but instead of hitting a lever with a mallet to see if he could ring the bell, Mike was hitting the tube with his breath to see if he could send the plunger to the top. Watching the plunger rise higher with each visit allowed the therapists to gauge how much improvement he was making. It was also meant to be a visual incentive to Mike.

A speech therapist began working with Mike each day, too, carefully monitoring his swallowing and trying to coax him to make noises. Swallowing requires a poetic degree of muscular coordination. If that coordination is compromised, even taking a sip of water becomes no small task. Forget about eating solids: not so much as a dollop of mashed potatoes can be conquered. Of course, food is life, so swallowing is a higher priority than talking, but the speech therapists were there to help with both.

The first speech therapist that came to visit Mike arrived with a tray of tools: a dentist's mirror, penlight, surgical gloves, and a cheery little pinwheel. The therapist explained that she was going to take a detailed inventory of Mike's mouth, tongue, lips, and larynx. And she did so just as thoroughly as if he were a car she were considering for purchase. This detailed assessment, called an Oral Mechanism Exam, is standard practice before speech therapy can begin.

"Mike, I'm going to look at your face and your mouth today to see how things are doing in there, okay?" she said. He stared and blinked slowly. "We want to make sure things are functioning properly."

The therapist began by checking the symmetry of Mike's face. No human face in the world is perfectly symmetrical, but what she was looking for was indication of one-sided weakness in the muscles. One side of Mike's face appeared a little slumped, one eyelid a little slacker than the other, but she didn't seem concerned.

Next she had him pucker his lips and fill his cheeks with air, making sure he could hold it for a few seconds without any leaking. He could. She asked him to smile. He didn't, not really.

She asked him to make the sounds OH, EE, OH, EE, OH, EE. He managed to produce a slurred version. She ran her fingers along his jawline, feeling for its shape and any damage. She asked him to open wide and shimmy his bottom jaw back and forth. "Doing great, Mike," she said as she wriggled her hand into a latex glove. "Now I want you to look at me and open your mouth really wide."

Mike moved slowly and was completely expressionless, but he complied. With the spirit in his eyes all but gone, it was as though she were inspecting a machine, not a man. And it was impossible for Brenda to get a read on how much he was understanding about the nature of this inspector's visit.

"I'm going to make sure everything's nice and pink and moist in here," the therapist continued. She shined the light inside his mouth. "Looks good."

Next, she asked him to stick out his tongue and wiggle it from side to side. It was a sight, a grown man who could not possibly look less amused, trying to mimic something from a children's playground game: *Neener, neener, neener!* He stuck out his tongue and moved it as instructed.

"You know when you get something sticky like peanut butter on the roof of your mouth?" she asked. "And you use your tongue to scrape it off? I want you to make that movement with your tongue right now." Again, he did so at a tortoise pace and with the enthusiasm of a wet towel. Peanut butter wouldn't have budged at the rate he was going, but at least he got the motion right.

After using a dental mirror to get a look at Mike's teeth, the therapist inspected his bite.

Then she shined her penlight in his mouth and pressed on his tongue with a depressor. "Good, Mike. You're doing great. The roof of your mouth looks healthy." Now she asked him to say, "Ah, ah, ah," as she watched to make sure the soft parts at the back of that roof moved up and down. They did. She checked his uvula and tonsils and the lingual frenulum, the narrow web of tissue that tethers the tongue to the floor of the mouth. Then she asked him to make a series of repetitive sounds as quickly as he could: *pah-pah-pah-pah* then *tah-tah-tah-tah*, then *kuh-kuh-kuh-kuh*. She might as well have asked him to recite "Peter Piper Picked a Peck of Pickled Peppers." It was clearly tough for him.

Finally, she grabbed the pinwheel and asked Mike to blow on it. What an odd sight: this trademark toy of childhood—so whimsical and cheery—rotating in front of Mike's dull gaze. His scruffy, slacken face looked so empty of feeling or thought, and the bright petals were still spinning, ever so slowly, as the therapist said, "Wonderful. We're all done for today."

By two weeks after he had been admitted to the hospital, the idea of Mike taking even a single step still seemed like pie in the sky. Yet Brenda remained faithfully optimistic that it would happen. The process just needed to be broken down into baby steps. After all, Mike hadn't so much as rolled over on his own in the bed, and most of his right side was out of commission.

The physical therapist that would help him with the baby steps was a brunette 30-something named Heather. She showed up just after Mike managed his first post-trauma bite of food. She was dressed in khaki slacks and a nautically colored sweater, looking every bit like a random stranger who just happened to come in on her lunch hour from some other job, at a school maybe, or a library. Definitely not a library: Heather had a solid voice that filled every inch of the air. It was gentle but firm, like a mother, and she talked with her whole face, too, raising her thick, black eyebrows as she spoke, gesticulating with hands that were lean and sinewy like the hands of someone who *work* worked.

"How are you doing today, Mike?" she asked. She even did the courtesy of waiting for him to answer, knowing he couldn't make the words and yet allowing for the possibility that he might. "I'm going to be working with you to see if we can't get you sitting up in a more comfortable position. Sound good?"

Mike held his stony gaze. Brenda patted him on the arm, exchanging a knowing look with Heather.

Mike's first attempt at sitting up was feeble at best, but Heather was kind and encouraging. She pulled him over to the side of the bed, lowered his legs to the floor, and released her hold on him, counting only a few seconds before he lost his balance and fell back on the bed as if drunk. She held him up a second time, and a third, and a fourth, before she stopped and promised to return in a little while.

"Good job today, Mike," she said as she was leaving. Brenda wondered what a bad job would look like.

Heather returned the next morning and repeated this exercise. Then she returned several times throughout the day to repeat it, like a trusty satellite that kept circling back. With each visit, with each attempt, Mike sat up for perhaps a second longer than his last try. By the end of the second day, after multiple sessions with Heather, Mike truly sat up for the first time.

Small victories gradually added up to hope, but there was so much uncertainty about whether and how Mike would be restored to his former self. He remained a far cry from it. All of his movements were in slow motion, but still, he was moving. Celebrating small victories for a man formerly capable of enormous ones, meant a huge shift in thinking, but Brenda and the kids went with it. They were sure God was working through Heather and the rest of the team.

Even though the Bible speaks of God healing all diseases, Brenda knew that everyone who prayed did not get healed. She believed that God was the source of all healing, but belief alone wasn't keeping her cup full. How could it? Everywhere she looked, she saw evidence of an interrupted life that once held a comfortable future. Piles of wind-tunnel schematics, family photographs on the dresser tops, notes from the women she had taught in her classes, a hammer laid atop an unfinished project in the woodshop, Mike's golf clubs, engineering books—these were brutal reminders of the amount of climbing left to do. Each one begged the question of just how many weeks, months, or years away they were from summiting the mountain.

From the beginning, they spoke to the mountain. They tried to pray it away. Their church demanded in continuous prayer that the Lord make the mountain fall away, but more and more, it seemed that "speaking to the mountain" wasn't as simple as all that. Maybe the crumbling came when one reached the summit. Maybe it eroded, grain by grain into the sea, over epochs unconcerned with our earthly timelines. Brenda couldn't know. She had to believe that God would reveal the meaning of that scripture in due time.

Each night, Brenda slept alone on her side of the bed, not daring to put so much as a foot on Mike's vacant side. She'd been wearing Mike's wedding band on a chain around her neck ever since it was removed in the hospital because his hands were a little swollen. In the darkness, under the covers, she pressed the ring between her fingers and tried to let sleep overcome her. Like a cruel monument, a pile of mail on the kitchen island grew higher by the inch every time Brenda passed it: the hospital bills and insurance correspondence began arriving almost from the first day of Mike's hospitalization and kept coming at an ever-increasing rate. Stephen was doing all he could to stay on top of them, but there was only so much that could be done.

Friends brought lots of food, which Brenda promptly didn't eat. She dared not say it to the good Samaritans who showed up, but the food piling up in the fridge irritated her. One more thing to do! She lost weight without even trying, and the skin under her eyes darkened as though in shadow. She didn't have the appetite for any of it, and being away from the hospital made her anxious, even though she desperately needed the breaks. She just didn't like not knowing *exactly* what was happening with Mike at every moment.

Each night when Brenda returned home, the empty lifelessness of her home was a harsh reminder of all the unknowns that stretched out before them. In a secret, secluded place in her heart, she wasn't totally sure how much distance Mike could cover and how much would remain out of reach for the rest of their lives. She tried not to look at that place in her heart, which was the mountain refusing to budge. Through prayer, she and her friends and family desperately hoped that they could truly command it to move.

10

But those who hope in the Lord will renew their strength. They will
soar on wings like eagles; they will run and not grow weary;
they will walk and not be faint.

— Isaiah 40:31 NIV —

In the late 80s, when Amanda was in the third grade and Stephen was in the fifth, Lockheed came to Mike with a proposition he couldn't refuse. The company was relocating its research and development department to a suburb of Los Angeles. Those in the department who were offered jobs, including Mike, had no choice but to move to California or find new work. At the time, the Palmers were still living in the future workshop they'd built with their own hands. The big home they'd intended to build on their parcel of land remained just a dream. Mike and Brenda flew out to Los Angeles to investigate the area and quickly discovered that the home prices were downright outlandish. To manage, they would need to live an absurd distance from the job and significantly downsize. That wasn't the only issue. The city just didn't feel right for two natives of the South who were so happily living in a simple town in Georgia.

Mike knew on the spot that the situation was a bad fit for his family, so he decided to leave Lockheed. Fortunately, he was quickly offered a job in Fort Worth, Texas, with General Dynamics, another aerospace and defense company. There, Mike would be working as a wind-tunnel test engineer on some landmark projects in the aerospace arena.

Part of Mike's new job would be conducting the hypersonic wind-tunnel tests needed for the National Aerospace Plane, or NASP. A hypersonic spaceplane manned by one person, the NASP would be able to travel to and from the earth's outer spheres just as an airplane might travel to and from New York. It was something NASA had been dreaming about since the launch of the first space shuttle five years prior, and in his 1986 State of the Union Address, President Ronald Reagan revealed that the federal government was working hard to make it a reality.

NASP was hailed by Reagan as "a new Orient Express that could, by the end of the next decade, take off from Dulles Airport and accelerate up to twenty-five times the speed of sound, attaining low-earth orbit or flying to Tokyo within two hours."

Moving away from Georgia was emotionally difficult, but the Palmers were a close-knit family and, as long as they had each other, they were unafraid of uprooting and starting fresh.

After they exchanged heart-wrenching goodbyes with their friends in Georgia, the family drove through a steely winter toward their new home in Texas. Their place in Texas was a small but new house in the bedroom community of Watauga, situated in the mid-cities between Fort Worth and Dallas. It was set on a corner lot with no sod, and whenever the cloudy skies shed their rain, the black Texas soil from the yard washed over the sidewalks like day-old coffee loosened from the bottom of a press. The place wasn't what they really wanted, but they never intended to stay in it or even Watauga for long. These were simply placeholders that would have to do until they sold their homes in Georgia—both the one they had built and the one they first lived in.

House in Texas

By then, Mike was so talented with his self-taught woodworking hobby, he could make just about anything from lumber. He enjoyed his hobby, and Brenda kept him busy with one project after another, so neither he nor Brenda gave a second thought to parking his workshop instead of their cars in the garage. They kept their cars on the driveway instead.

The Texas winter was windy and often cold, with temperatures that spiked and plummeted erratically. The mercury would climb to seventy degrees one day but visit the 30-degree hatch mark the next. Brenda was grateful she could drive the kids to school, though it was just a mile away, so that they didn't have to walk or wait at a bus stop in such unpredictable climes.

One day, when Mike was on a business trip, an ice storm hit. Brenda found that her car wouldn't start when it was time to get the kids from school. She scrambled out and into their other car, but it wouldn't start either. The cold wind was blowing hard, and the sky was spewing sleet, but being new to town, Brenda had nobody she could call for help. She threw on a coat and started walking to the school instead. As she trudged along, a car slowly rolled up alongside her.

Through a rolled-down window, a kind woman with a Texas drawl politely asked Brenda if she might like a ride. She took Brenda to retrieve the kiddos and back home again. Brenda was thankful, but the experience made her painfully aware of her lack of local connections.

Brenda missed her Georgia friends terribly. She was lonely for that comfortable and easy companionship she had with Bernie. Each day, she pleaded in prayer that she would find new friends in her new community. It didn't help that Mike had to travel often for his job. She tried to lean heavily on God as a reminder that she was never truly alone, but she craved the closeness of missing friendships.

Though this vacuum and the beginning of the move were hard, it didn't take long for the whole family to fall in love with Texans. They seemed such genuine, down-home folk with no hidden agendas. Brenda was tickled by how much Texans loved their state, many of them flying humongous Texas and American flags in their yards or in front of their businesses. And whenever she was the one traveling, Brenda loved stepping off the plane back in Dallas and seeing authentic cowboys in their distinctive boots and 10-gallon hats.

Many weekends, the family drove to the Stockyards in Fort Worth to see the rodeo. The Stockyards were bustling with all the trappings of an old western cow town, which is exactly what the place used to be. There were stagecoach rides and swinging saloon doors, old-time photo studios and shops stocked with spurs, bolo ties, and gaudy, oversized belt buckles.

Costumed *vaqueros* made a show of longhorn cattle-drive demonstrations down the main drag. The glowering beasts walked with their heads hung low, their grand and elegant horns curling out like God's ironworks from their temples in the shape of yawning script *W*s. That year, there was a contest underway at the Stockyards to win a Dodge truck.

Participants had to coast a certain number of paper airplanes into the bed of a pickup truck that was parked in the center of the arena each week. Crisp white sheets of paper were passed out at the door, so people could write their names on their papers, fold them into planes, and try to aim their creations into the truck bed. Amanda and Stephen were mightily impressed with the airplanes their dad made. Unsurprising for an aerospace engineer, he crafted sleek, sharp-nosed beauties that seemed to glide directly into the truck bed. Also unsurprising, at the end of the contest season, Mike received free tickets to the Stockyards along with a note that he was being entered into the drawing for the truck. He didn't win the truck, but his kids were awfully proud.

Family vacation to Colorado

By far, the family's favorite thing about living in Texas was Restoration Church. At the time, evangelical churches all across the country were going through a "Charismatic awakening." The Charismatic movement among Protestant churches began back in the 1960s, but it was only now that it was truly catching fire. Brenda and Mike had been exposed to the tradition years earlier at retreats they attended in Alabama on the recommendation of some friends. Those retreats were led by Dudley Hall, a gifted teacher and trailblazer of the charismatic awakening. He also happened to be a teacher at Restoration Church. Now, each Sunday, they heard compelling teaching and preaching in the morning from the church's pastor, Doug White, and then again in the evening from Dudley.

Even though they were veterans of Dudley's retreats, nothing they saw at those seminars really prepared them for the experience of attending this large, "shopping-center church." It felt so alive with expressive worship and preaching, and the resounding message of grace and freedom through knowing Jesus Christ filled them with a newfound sense of wonder and joy. Though both were Christians from as far back as they could remember, this was the first time in their lives they could barely wait to go to church, and they easily formed a strong friendship with Dudley.

One of the first Sundays Mike and Brenda attended Restoration Church, they stopped to read a bulletin board pinned with information about all the small groups that met throughout the city. Dudley walked up to the board and pointed to one of the groups and said, "You guys need to join that group."

The first group meeting they attended was held at the home of a couple named Rick and Mary. As soon as they walked in the door, both Mike and Brenda felt at home. A stout pot of coffee and a pretty quilt of desserts was the hub around which the group was gathered in enthusiastic conversation. Brenda wasn't a coffee-drinker, but Mary said, "Let me fix you a cup of coffee you will love." She proceeded to assault a cup of coffee with so much cream and sugar, it might as well have been hot chocolate. But she was right: Brenda loved the sweet concoction and became a lifelong coffee-drinker on the spot.

There was laughing, easy conversation, and a sense of warmth as the group gathered every week. To a person, they were all friendly and embraced Mike and Brenda from the start. Many would become some of the Palmers' closest friends.

Along with the Charismatic tradition sweeping over the church came a change in the type of worship music. Gone were the robed choir numbers bookended by the shrill voices of soprano ladies and the deep-earth voices of baritones. No more traditional hymns piped through organs or plinked out on pianos. These were replaced with guitars and drums, loudspeakers, and screens with the lyrics projected on them. *Choir directors* became *praise leaders.*

Many of the Palmers' new friends were frustrated choir members who missed their choir days. Brenda helped by sitting down at the piano at the beginning of each group meeting, with everyone gathering around to sing a combination of new praise songs and old hymns. She loved seeing the looks on their faces as the soft pads of her fingertips worked the cool, smooth keys with songs they knew by heart.

Despite it all—the rodeo and the Stockyards, the exciting church, and the easy friendships—the constant travel required of Mike for his job made Texas living tough. He was frequently gone for stretches of at least two weeks, but usually three or four, to conduct wind-tunnel tests. Brenda deeply missed him and felt exhausted and lonely. About one-third of her life was now spent as a *de facto* single parent. Mike was no happier about the situation, and before long, they were in agreement that Texas was not right for their family. Yet they couldn't move again until the year was up: Mike's contract dictated that if he did, he would have to reimburse the company for moving expenses. When the year was up, they were off again.

The Palmers' next destination was Huntsville, Alabama, a town nicknamed "Rocket City" for its close history with US space missions. Mike took a position with Micro Craft, a smaller operation that specialized in the design and fabrication of wind-tunnel models for NASA. He was hired to manage the company's three-year contract with Marshall Space Flight Center on the Space Shuttle Main Engine (SSME). He was also to conduct wind-tunnel testing of the solid rocket booster model for the space shuttle launch system. Not a lot of people can say their job is rocket science. Mike could.

The job carried a lot of pressure and responsibility, and Mike frequently had to drive to the company's home office ninety minutes away. Plus, he and Brenda now had *three* houses to sell—two in Georgia, and one in Texas. They took a rental home while they waited for buyers. Once they unloaded the Texas home, about a year later, they were able to buy a place in Huntsville.

The search for a new church was on again, but they couldn't manage to find one that was quite like the one they so loved in Texas. Instead, they narrowed in on two churches and regularly attended first one, then the other. The first church was not a good fit. At the second church, the entire family played together in a worship band—Brenda on keyboard, Mike on guitar, Stephen on drums, and Amanda on flute.

The kids were starting to come into their own, showing little signs of the adults they would one day shape up to be. Both became active in middle school band, formed close friendships, and did well in classes. A cocker spaniel was given to them around this time, their first family pet. The kids named him Charlie, and he quickly became a beloved family member.

One evening, Mike came home with a story about an unusual event that had happened at work that day. Apparently, an entrepreneur had gotten hold of a professional reference book that listed MicroCraft as being linked to wind tunnels, and then reached out to the company for help with a wild idea that was promptly forwarded to Mike, the resident wind-tunnel expert. The proposition amused him, but he didn't give it much serious thought: The entrepreneur was passionately interested in developing a mobile indoor skydiving wind tunnel that could be moved around to traveling amusement carnivals. His name was Bill Kitchen.

11

Pain is a kindly, hopeful thing, a certain proof of life, a clear assurance that all is not yet over, that there is still a chance.

— A. J. Gossip —

One afternoon, Brenda had the random and startling realization while driving home that she was now responsible for keeping the family car in good repair. Never before had she been responsible for a car, seldom even putting gas in one. No, Mike did that. Though technically a small matter by comparison to the rest of what was happening in her life, the car suddenly seemed a burden too large. A few nights later, she noticed that a shelf bracket holding the TV receiver was broken. *I better get Mike to fix that,* she thought, only to remember he couldn't—not now and maybe not ever. Then, as she walked up the stairs to the bedroom afterward, a stunning thought popped into her mind: *sex might never be a part of her life again either.* Exhausted, she climbed into bed, turned out the light, and fell asleep looking at Mike's pillow next to her.

Everywhere she turned, there was *one more thing.*

With Mike's condition still serious and extremely altered, Brenda made up her mind to celebrate each improvement, no matter how small. Over the days to come, tiny steps turned into slightly less tiny steps, resulting in Mike being able to do things like use his own hands to eat and drink—just his left hand, because he still wasn't using his right arm. Once he got pretty good at it, Brenda brought him a banana to see how he'd peel it. Would it compel him to try out that right arm or perhaps even attempt to speak to get help? Instead, ever the problem solver, Mike studied the thing for a few seconds, slowly brought it to his mouth, and began peeling it with his teeth. *Of course!*

Brenda thought. *A most logical solution!* That was just so Mike, and that, in and of itself, was a victory all its own.

Coffee had been part of Mike's normal daily routine at home, and Brenda wasn't sure if he could steady a cup of hot liquid in his hand, but she figured the only way to find out was to try. So, later that morning, she sat a cup of it in front of him on the hospital tray and anxiously waited to see what he would do. She felt victorious as she watched him simply reach for it, even though he picked it up with his non-dominant hand, the only working hand he had for the moment. She was delighted to see him sip from the cup in the same familiar way he always had. It was more evidence to her that the old Mike was still there. Brenda settled into a routine of arriving by 8 a.m. each morning, often stopping at Starbucks on the way. She seriously doubted that Mike noticed the difference between the cheap hospital coffee and his fancy Starbucks, but the stop was therapeutic for Brenda. Walking among the ordinary, going to a place where average customers were stopping on their way to work, helped her regain a sense of her life being less altered than it was.

Of those who came to the hospital, Brenda was selective about who she brought to Mike's bedside. She felt a keen responsibility to protect his dignity, sensing in her gut how to know the ones he really should see and the ones who just wanted to see him. She was more at ease allowing in people who were closest to him, especially men and friends who were familiar with all things medical.

Libby was a dental surgical nurse, and she stopped by the hospital one day on her way home from work, wearing surgical scrubs. During Libby's visit, Brenda decided to do a little experiment. She started by laying out some coins on Mike's tray.

"Mike, can you show me the penny?" They waited.

"Can you show me the nickel?" They waited.

"How about the dime...or the quarter?"

They both watched with aching hearts as Mike aimlessly moved the coins around on the tray with his left hand, either not caring or unable to point out which were which. It was one of countless moments in step-down that Brenda found nightmarish. Seeing her brilliant husband unable to comprehend even the simplest things was deeply painful. However, it was by continually attempting these exercises that she believed she would gradually see proof of progress.

Just as in the ICU, Brenda was seldom alone in the waiting area when she left Mike's bedside and was instead surrounded by a continuous and welcome stream of friends. Some of them stopped only briefly, not sure what to do or say. Others appeared completely at ease and came with a sense of purpose, as if on a mission, wanting to read a scripture or say something specific that was on their hearts. By now, Mike was beginning to show some recognition of the select few visitors that Brenda brought to his room. He responded by staring at them and obeying simple requests to squeeze their hands. Occasionally, he even attempted to say their names, but the effect was only moans and groans, not speech.

Joe and Robin came regularly, sometimes more than once a day. Stan stopped by Mike's room throughout the day as his hospital duties allowed. He noticed every little improvement, no matter how small, and excitedly pointed them out at every opportunity. He spoke to Mike in the same tone and manner that he always had, careful to focus on the positive. Brenda deeply appreciated these visitors. Their presence helped her to know she and Mike were not alone on this painful walk, and it gave her the sense that these friends were battling alongside them, holding them up through moments of the most intense weakness.

The nursing staff was, of course, vitally important to Mike's recovery, and Brenda considered them to be competent, caring professionals. But on her arrival one morning, all the nurses were busy helping a belligerent patient in the next bed who was fighting against the insertion of a tracheal tube.

Mike was lying in a bed of urine-soaked sheets, flat on his back, staring at the ceiling. Judging by his appearance, Brenda could only conclude he had been neglected for quite some time. She felt an intense rage and the urge to scream at the nurses, a reaction completely out of character for her, but at that moment, she wasn't concerned about decorum. She wasn't concerned about anything other than Mike's condition and care.

Before she had a chance to erupt in anger, Amanda intervened and assured her mom that the problem would be handled.

"Just wait here, Mom," she instructed. "Stay calm. I'll take care of it."

Amanda went in search of a young nurse she had seen earlier, one who also happened to be a member of Brenda and Mike's church. This nurse was responsible for an entirely different part of that floor of the hospital, but at Amanda's request, she came right away and tended to Mike's situation, cleaning him up and making sure he was comfortable before she made sure Brenda and Amanda were okay, too. Her kindness was a balm to Brenda's spirit that she would never forget.

Still, Brenda could not be put at ease for long. So, Mike wasn't lying in a pool of his own urine anymore. Fine. What of the fact that he wet the bed at all? What of the reality that he couldn't ask for help and wasn't able to get to a bathroom if his life depended on it? And how strange to realize that these were all relatively minor problems on the tip of a very large iceberg made of much scarier problems.

The rest of that iceberg kept Brenda from ever fully relaxing and feeling peace. Of particular concern was the fact that Mike still wasn't talking at all. Brenda was warned early on by Dr. Adam that the brain surgery would remove only the anomaly and clot, not fix any damage already done by them. More specifically, she was informed that speech and language were the major question marks and cause for concern, since the area of the brain that controls these skills was the one that suffered the most bleeding. She was warned that potential outcomes for Mike were all over the map, from total speech loss, to being unable to make any sense when he spoke, to being unable to comprehend what other people were saying. Despite these warnings, Brenda was not prepared for him to be mute.

One day, when Dr. Adam was making his rounds, Brenda shared how frustrating and worrisome it was, this waiting and wondering to see if Mike would ever talk again.

"What has he said so far?" the doctor asked.

"Nothing, really."

Dr. Adam reached up, placed his hand on Mike's shoulder blade, and dug his fingers into Mike's flesh, causing him to squirm in pain.

"What's your name?" he asked in a firm tone. The message was clear, that he wouldn't release his death grip until he got what he was looking for.

"MIKE." He answered with no hesitation at all and total clarity.

Dr. Adam looked at Brenda and said in a matter-of-fact voice, "He can talk."

The speech therapist later explained the concept of *reflexive verbal response*. Many patients who are otherwise nonverbal will respond to painful stimuli with a word or string of words they've used frequently in life. These are usually words from situations your average person encounters on a regular basis, such as being asked how they are or told, "I love you." Therefore, words like *fine* and *love you too* are among the things otherwise nonverbal patients are likely to blurt when some doctor comes along and claws into their muscles. It's not that the patient has been resisting speech until then. It's that these words are reflexes, stored far deeper in the brain than other words they know, somewhere within the limbic system. The limbic system is where people house their emotional selves, and it's largely where memories are formed. The motor pathways to words stored in the limbic system are roads well-traveled.

Brenda was stunned. Mike was a talker, and now she had proof that he could still speak but was battling some hurdle in the brain that held him back. She now better grasped the warnings Dr. Adam gave her before Mike's surgery, his prediction that speech could be compromised in some way, but only time would tell if or how. This was Brenda's first real glimpse at the complex layers involved in the act of speaking. She was going to see that speech isn't a mere matter of *talks* or *doesn't talk*. There are shades of gray, small pieces that join to finally produce speech. For Mike, it was as if the starter on a car's engine were broken, but the engine itself was not. That made perfect sense based on the particulars of his brain injury.

Imaging showed that one area of Mike's brain that was affected by the bleed was near something the doctors described as a supplementary motor area. Indeed, it's the place that causes people to initiate almost any action, the area where *thinking* about something evolves into *doing* that thing, so it's where you'll find the ON switch for anything related to speech. Armed with proof that Mike had the *ability* to talk, Brenda became obsessed with coaxing him to do so, trying to discover things that would give him the jump-start he seemed to need. Mike used to drive a car that had a stick shift, and if that car didn't start, it was a blessing to be parked on a hill, facing downward.

He would put the car in gear, turn on the ignition, and press on the clutch. When the car had momentum, he would let out the clutch and voilá, the engine roared up. That's what Brenda wanted to do with his speech—get him rolling down the hill so he could talk. She so missed hearing his voice and the give-and-take of conversation with him. How could she could make him talk without inflicting pain on him? She felt she would, of course, resort to hurting Mike if that was the only thing that would work, but there had to be other ways.

Brenda noticed that when anyone called on the phone and wanted to say something to Mike, he would at least make noises, as opposed to not making any attempt at all. So, she arranged for Amanda to be in Mike's room while Brenda called him from a phone outside the hospital. She then pleaded with him over the phone to please, please, please say something to her, anything at all. Her begging was enough to get him to respond with grunts and other vaguely verbal sounds. Though this was a tiny step, it's one that again confirmed Mike's ability to speak. He would do it given the right stimulus, so Brenda allowed herself to feel hopeful that his language skills would be fully restored.

Speech was only part of the equation, of course, and with each new victory came a reminder that there were a thousand yet to be conquered. Some of these challenges were much bigger than others, like walking. Such monolithic hurdles were difficult for Brenda to mentally narrow down into bite-size pieces that wouldn't overwhelm her thinking, though the medical staff tried to parse them down when they explained the work they were doing with Mike.

Brenda had faith he'd walk and was told it was reasonable to continue having it, but as with everything else in his recovery, she couldn't be sure what degree of success he'd achieve. She also couldn't know how long it would take for him to achieve any one success, and whether they had to be conquered in succession or if they might come all at once. But if a man couldn't even sit up without collapsing like a scarecrow off the stick one day, how many more days, weeks, months or, God forbid, years might it take for him to walk again?

By now, Mike indeed was able to sit up a bit, and Heather, the physical therapist, was determined that walking would be his next victory. She told the family it likely would be an extremely slow process, one that needed to be done in very small increments. Brenda thought of the old saying about a watched pot never boiling and imagined this wait would prove a thousand times longer, maybe like watching an empty swimming pool fill up with drizzling rain.

Each new rehabilitation project was complicated by the fact of Mike's deficits in speech and language, and the mystery of their exact nature. After all, he needed to comprehend what was being said to him in order to comply with certain therapies. *Mike, can you show me the penny...the nickel...the dime... the quarter?* Any time he didn't comply with requests, the question loomed: Is it that he can't do it, that he won't do it, or that he doesn't comprehend what's being said? And because Mike remained expressionless, his eyes flat and dull, it was nearly impossible to read his face for clues. Heather was good at her job and accustomed to just this sort of thing. She began each walking session with Mike by putting a sort of thick cloth belt around his waist, a little like the *obi*, or belt, on a Japanese kimono. She used it like a harness, something she could grip to keep his movements steadier.

From the beginning of these sessions, it was clear that Mike could step with only his left leg. Nobody was surprised this was the case, based on the lack of movement he'd shown on his right side throughout his hospitalization. Mike dutifully complied with Heather's instructions that he take his steps, lifting his left foot and setting it down in front of him without issue.

However, she then had to sort of push his right leg from behind to *make* it take its turn, something she did while holding onto the cloth around his waist. This step-pushing procedure gradually increased in length of minutes upon each of her visits. In the days to come, it would eventually grow into a step-shuffling set of movements that led Mike from his room and right into the hospital hallway and beyond.

Mothers might recognize something familiar in this walking maneuver. There's a little trick of circling a belt or scarf around a near-toddler's chest and under the armpits, giving the parent something to grasp to hold the child steady during the child's early attempts to walk.

When it's a toddler at the end of the tether, each drunken step is celebrated, by parent and child alike. When it's a grown man, any joy felt at witnessing the drunken steps is counterweighted with the sadness of all that's been lost in the first place. Yes, Mike was kind of sort of beginning to walk, but just a couple of weeks earlier, he had been able to run, golf, make love, build prototypes, and climb ladders. His unsteady steps were a reminder that basic skills, a whole lifetime's worth of them, were wiped out by that nasty snarl of vessels no bigger than a quarter.

Truth be told, Brenda was thrilled just to see Mike in a standing position, shaky though he was. She thought of each small step as forward movement, not just literally but figuratively. Only a few weeks were behind them in the hospital now, but it felt to her as though she hadn't seen Mike standing up in a very long time. How tall he seemed!

As he neared his third week in the hospital, Mike's days of recovery took on a degree of predictability, with the same people coming and going at fixed intervals. All were trying to work into place their respective puzzle pieces. Mike wasn't saying much. He was barely eating. He couldn't do basic arithmetic. He couldn't hold a pencil, or do much else, with his dominant hand. Though Heather had already helped him learn to sit up and even take a few steps, thus far she'd lent him the strength and balance of her own body in the process, pushing his right leg forward for him and holding him steady with that sash around his waist. Much of the right side of his body remained useless or weak. He had a long way to go.

12

Remember not the former things, nor consider the things of old. Behold,
I am doing a new thing; now it springs forth, do you not perceive it?
I will make a way in the wilderness and rivers in the desert.
— Isaiah 43:18-19 ESV —

Mike had been in the step-down unit for close to a week when the head of the hospital's satellite rehab facility, a kind gentleman by the name of Dr. Mark Ross, began visiting him every couple of days. Mike's doctor requested these visits, explaining to the family that, once he met certain milestones, Mike would be discharged into a rehab center. Namely, he would need to be off most of his medications and no longer tethered to a catheter. Brenda was still feeling shell-shocked and couldn't even begin to imagine Mike leaving the hospital. His condition remained so untenable to her that she just couldn't see a way out. Dr. Ross helped a little with the anxiety by being gentle and kind and always keeping things positive when he checked on Mike's neurological and physical progress.

"Soon," he said one day. "We'll be able to transfer him soon."

It was then that it struck her: one of these days, somehow, she would not walk out to her car alone at the end of the day but would instead have Mike with her, perhaps in a wheelchair, perhaps not. And together they would drive to their house in Poquoson under the tall, tall trees. The kids would say their goodbyes and head back to their own lives in faraway towns. Brenda would wave to them as they drove away. Would Mike be able to do the same? She would walk back in the house, close the door, and then it would be just the two of them again. How different would their life be? She couldn't begin to fathom it.

The next time their friend Joe came to visit Mike at the hospital, Brenda brought up the possibility of Mike's eventual homecoming. She didn't know when it would be, but she knew for certain now that it was coming.

"I'll see to it that we get wheelchair ramps built if he needs them," Joe said. His reaction took Brenda by surprise. She had never considered such a thing! Of course, ramps would be necessary if Mike didn't make further progress with his walking. Every day, their strange new reality shook her up in one way or another.

One afternoon, Dr. Adam unceremoniously announced that it was time for the family to decide on a rehab facility. Afterward, a patient advocate explained to them that it was standard procedure for a patient's insurance company to receive updates on the needs of the patient and agree to treatment, week by week. At this point, Mike's policy would allow the family to choose any rehab facility they wanted in the state of Virginia. It would be covered just as the hospital was covered, giving Brenda and the kids quite a bit of latitude in their decision-making.

Since the family was already familiar with Dr. Ross, they decided to investigate his facility first. He was the head of Riverside Rehabilitation, the rehab center affiliated with the hospital, and Brenda arranged for Amanda to visit that center on her own. It did not go well.

When Amanda returned from her tour, she was seething. She said that the head nurse at the facility was some sort of fatalist, punctuating the entire tour with ominous commentary on Mike's condition.

"She said that if he isn't walking by now, he probably never will. And if he isn't talking by now, he'll most likely never do that either."

Amanda's blue eyes were steely as she relayed the story and swallowed back tears.

Brenda was equally shaken. Because she had faith in God's healing, she believed Mike would walk and talk again, but a big part of her needed other people to believe it, too, particularly those who would be caring for him. Amanda didn't wait for Brenda to cast the verdict. She had one of her own: "I absolutely do not want Dad in that place."

The next time Dr. Adam came to visit Mike's room, Brenda and Amanda shared with him the story of what the rehab nurse had said. He made no effort to disguise his shock, and soon after contacted Dr. Ross to let him know the situation. Dr. Ross wasted no time making amends. The very next day, he made a personal visit to Mike's room to apologize to the family. He also asked Brenda if she would consider allowing him a chance to personally tour her around the facility. She reluctantly agreed.

When Brenda went to the facility, leaving Amanda behind with Mike, she was prepared to not like it, but Dr. Ross did a stellar job of mending the situation. He showed Brenda the entire facility, from top to bottom, and gave her personal assurance that the family would be happy with it.

As far as appearances go, the building wasn't anything dazzling. It had big, wide windows, friendly enough nurses, brightly painted walls, a room stocked with games and puzzles—but there was no covering up the fact that this was a place where broken bodies were sent to work. With linoleum floors, fluorescent lighting, walkers, canes, and wheelchairs, and a rickety elevator that traversed four small floors, the place was decidedly clinical.

The thing that Brenda most liked about Riverside Rehab was its location. From the outside, the drab white building—blockish and severe, with vertical windows that were as narrow as floor planks—had the air of a minimum-security jail, but from the inside, on each of the four floors, the clinic boasted a majestic view of the beautiful Chesapeake Bay through the banks of windows on the east. There was even a rooftop patio on an eastern segment of the second floor. As Brenda gazed out over the water, summer winds combed across its surface, puckering it up into tiny meringue whitecaps that glistened in the sun. In the distance, she could see the iconic shipyards jutting out on their little peninsula, a jagged silhouette of massive cranes and behemoth ships. "Can you assure me Mike will have one of the rooms on the water side of the building?" Brenda asked Dr. Ross. In her mind's eye, she could see Mike sitting on that patio overlooking the water. Maybe it would do him some good.

Though Dr. Ross gave Brenda his assurances, she and Amanda decided to delay their decision so they could visit two other rehab centers, both in Richmond, more than an hour from Brenda's and Mike's home. One of the facilities was a large inner-city hospital. The other was a new place situated out in the country with a beautiful pastoral setting.

Somewhere in the back of Brenda's mind, she remembered Mike's voice in the days just before his brain bleed. "I've got to get the car out for new tires," he had said. Brenda knew that Mike would want those tires changed before she took a road trip to Richmond, especially if they ended up putting him in a facility that far from home. She knew those tires *needed* to be changed if Mike said so. With a pit in her stomach, she also knew it was her responsibility now to keep up the cars, their yard, their home, their bills—their life. When a friend came to visit Mike that afternoon and asked what he could do to help, Brenda said, "Tires." She gave him the keys to the car and a check, and he took care of the rest, looking grateful for the chance to make even a little difference during this awful time for his friends.

The trip to the facility in Richmond was uninspiring, making it somewhat easy for Brenda to make her choice. It just *felt* wrong. The country facility was picturesque enough to be tempting but not enough to compete with the biggest thing Riverside Rehab had going for it, which was not the bay view or Dr. Ross but the proximity to the family's huge support network of friends. All those friends that were still steadily visiting Mike and Brenda at the hospital were significant. Their presence mattered. It wasn't merely symbolic. It was a form of energy that added something to Mike's healing, something real and palpable. Even Dr. Adam made no bones about telling Brenda how important it was to Mike's recovery that he remain near friends during rehab. He warned Brenda that people do not tend to travel great distances to call on friends who are hospitalized for any length of time. She took his words to heart and made the decision to go with Riverside.

Before transferring to the rehab center, Mike was moved into a private room at the hospital for a few days. The 24-hour nursing staff that vigilantly orbited his world in step-down was no more. Brenda felt the weight of responsibility shifting onto her shoulders now. She could still get nursing help, but it was greatly reduced.

Amanda continued to insist that Brenda go home and rest at night. Amanda appeared to have bottomless patience, and the wheels in her mind seemed to be constantly turning as she held her nighttime vigil, seeking logical ways to help move the recovery process along. Even the little things helped. One morning, Brenda arrived to find Mike lying on his side instead of flat on his back. He'd been on his back for the entire three weeks of his hospital stay! During the night, Amanda had come up with a way he could roll into another position by pulling himself over with the side rails. Something about the sight gave Brenda a little relief, knowing how good it must feel to Mike to be able to lie in a different position after all that time. Yes, the little things weren't little at all. Later that morning, waiting to see if the transfer order would turn up at any second, Brenda decided to put on some praise music with lyrics instead of just peaceful instrumental music. Upon hearing the words, Mike began to cry. That wasn't like him. It seemed to Brenda that the words touched something beyond the physical, as though they were permeating deep places in her husband's soul that were aching to be reached. There was a supernatural quality to his response, a stirring of something way down. Words were still not possible for Mike, but in that moment, they also weren't necessary. Brenda reached out a hand and laid it across Mike's. Together, they let the music wash over them.

13

I wait for the Lord, my soul waits, and in his word I hope.
— Psalm 130:5 NKJV —

Father's Day arrives each year on the third Sunday in June, and weeks before Mike collapsed in his office, Brenda had purchased an expensive writing pen that she planned to give him for the occasion. It was a gleaming metal number that felt substantial in the hand, the sort that belonged on a big mahogany desk next to an art-glass paperweight. The clerk told her to come back after Mike opened the gift, said the store would engrave his signature into the side of the pen. Of course, Father's Day fell twenty-five days after Mike's brain bleed rendered his right hand unusable. He could no more write his autograph than he could hop out of bed and do an Irish jig. Stephen couldn't be there that Father's Day, because he was on a brief stint to Texas to pack more clothes and to hammer out the arrangements for an extended leave of absence. So, on that third Sunday in June, Amanda and Brenda sat together with Mike, watching as he held his absurd new gift in his left hand and vacantly scribbled on paper like a child. It was a bleak sight.

By this time, Mike was able to hold himself in a sitting position without assistance and was no longer tethered to a catheter, so he was allowed to be taken out for short trips around the hospital in a wheelchair. He was also taking short steps, though still with a considerable amount of help from Heather, the physical therapist. Those things that needed to be done before he could be released to the rehab center were now done. The family was told to prepare.

Before leaving the hospital that night, Brenda and Amanda had a painfully honest discussion that was begging to be had.

"I don't even know if he really knows who we are, Mom."

"Neither do I."

"It could be he's responding to us just because we're the ones who've been with him since he woke up. Maybe he's just gotten used to us being there."

Brenda's heart ached at the thought. It wasn't the first time it occurred to her, but she had been plunging that fear down deep every time it tried to come creeping up. It was just too disturbing to imagine, and wasn't the Lord at work here? Because Mike still wasn't speaking, all she had to go on were his facial expressions, which remained dull and lifeless, and his compliance with simple commands, such as squeezing a hand when asked to do so. He gave little indication that he recognized anyone from before the brain injury. The conversation with Amanda left Brenda feeling deeply troubled. On her drive home, she mentally replayed it over and over. She always knew Amanda to be a good judge of situations, level-headed and objective, so she put a lot of trust in her daughter's perspective and instincts. Simply knowing Amanda was fearing the same things, having those same disturbing thoughts, made the possibility of their truth more real. But knowing she wasn't alone with these dark concerns didn't make Brenda feel any less alone. In fact, she was lonelier than ever now. She missed Mike so much, she physically hurt, and now her greatest fear—his absence—was brought to the fore.

The next day was transfer day, a graduation of sorts. Brenda approached it with a mix of trepidation and thanksgiving. There were just so many unknowns. Only three and a half weeks had passed since Mike's AVM rupture. It felt like an eternity, but Brenda was far from acclimated. Almost everything happening felt unfamiliar to her, and rehab would mean transferring to another foreign place. Fears aside, it was time. Dr. Adam told them he wanted to see Mike in his office in one month if he was out of the rehabilitation center by then. Otherwise, he would come to Mike.

It was a cloudy, drizzly morning. Amanda was home, resting after her nightly vigil. Stephen was still in Texas. Brenda sat alone with Mike in the quiet room, waiting for him to be retrieved for the ride to his new home away from home. The occasion did not feel joyous.

Eventually, two EMTs came to the room to prepare him. First, they wrapped him in his hospital bedding and moved him to the gurney, which was cushioned with sheets, blankets, and pillows. Then they fastened a series of straps around his body before wheeling him from the room. Mike looked like a human burrito tucked into a linen tortilla. Brenda joked to the EMTs that she hoped they planned on driving carefully. That got a little chuckle out of them.

Outside, Brenda was told to drive behind the ambulance to follow it to the rehabilitation facility. As she walked across the black pavement of the parking lot, she finally was able to fully take in the gravity of the moment. This move was a huge milestone. Mike hadn't died. He lived. He hadn't stayed in a coma. He woke up. He wasn't done recovering. He was going to a place that was all about hope for more improvement. Could the worst be behind her now? She didn't feel that way.

A heavy summer rain was falling all around Newport News that day. It must have been nearly noon, and as Brenda followed the ambulance out of the parking lot, her windshield wipers slapped out a comforting rhythm. The ambulance drove slowly, lights and sirens turned off. It made a few turns on city streets before heading down a straight stretch of highway. What happened next was like a movie playing in slow motion before Brenda's eyes.

First, a car pulled too closely in front of the ambulance. The ambulance driver responded by swerving to the right. The ambulance fishtailed. Coming out of one swerve, it went careening up onto a curb and smashed directly into a large wooden post. A huge green sign that was attached to the post was knocked free and went soaring backward, flying right over the top of Brenda's car. As it passed over her head, she read the words *JAMES RIVER BRIDGE*.

As the sign sailed past, Brenda heard in almost audible words, "Satan tried to kill Mike once, and now he's trying again, but he won't be able to do it." She was sure these weren't her words because there was simply no time for her to formulate them. A sense of peace and calmness washed over her as she watched the ambulance come to a bouncing stop on top of the median.

Brenda pulled her car in front of the ambulance and reached for her phone to call 911, but in her rear-view mirror, she could see that the passenger EMT was already making a call, and then the thought occurred to her: *They are 911!* So, she jumped out of her vehicle and hurried through the driving rain back to the driver's side door of the ambulance. She swung his door open and saw that his head was bleeding and slumped against the steering wheel. He appeared to be unconscious.

"Can you hold his head steady while I grab a neck brace?" the other EMT asked as he clamored to the back of the ambulance. Brenda climbed in next to the driver and cupped her hands on either side of his bleeding head. He was coming to.

"Is my husband okay?" she called to the other EMT as he rummaged for a neck brace. Having watched the men wrap up and strap Mike into that padded gurney back at the hospital, Brenda really didn't feel any sense of panic. She was sure his bed was safely secured to the ambulance floor, too. The EMT gave her a nod that told her Mike was fine. Brenda looked back to the injured driver, whose head she still cupped firmly between her hands. She felt utterly calm and confident as she began speaking to him in her soft Southern drawl.

"You're fine," she said. "It's okay. I know how to pray."

Brenda was in familiar territory. She asked the driver for his name, and then she began to pray for him, calling him by name. She continued her prayer until a passerby stopped to see if he could help. As the man approached the ambulance, the other EMT asked him to take Brenda's place.

"Can you take over and hold his head steady, just like she's doing?" he asked. Then he looked at Brenda. "You can come on back here to be with your husband."

Brenda walked around to the back and stepped up into the ambulance. She found Mike just as she thought she'd find him: completely secure, wrapped in his hospital bedding. But he looked up at Brenda with the most wide-eyed amazement. He looked startled.

Reaction! Emotion! Awareness!

"Mike, this wasn't supposed to be part of the ride," Brenda reassured him. Then she sat down beside his bed, flipped open her cell phone, and dialed a number. "Amanda, it's me. You will *not* believe what just happened."

Two other ambulances arrived at the scene in short order, one for Mike, and the other for the injured EMT. Knowing her help was no longer needed, Brenda calmly walked back to her car in the rain, started the engine, and navigated herself through the short drive that remained to Riverside Rehabilitation. There, she waited by the front door.

Soon, the ambulance pulled up under the concrete awning of the building. When the EMTs rolled Mike out the rear doors, Brenda saw that his salt-and-pepper hair was wet, and the rest of him was soaked to the bone. That's what happens when you're transferred out of a crashed ambulance on the highway in the driving rain.

14

No person, not even the best one, can give your soul all it needs.
— Tim Keller —

Despite having a starring role in the Christian narrative, Satan is kept boxed up in the attic of the belief systems of many modern churchgoers. He's an odd relic that gets trotted out during, say, Thursday night Bible study, which is no wonder. Mixed company isn't likely to blink at the mention of God, but talk of a sadistic, immortal being that can cause bad things to happen (and, oh, by the way, take the shape of a serpent) is kind of a brow-raiser.

Not for Brenda. From as far back as memory could take her, Brenda was fed a steady diet of old-time religion. It was the evangelical variety, "tried in the fiery furnace" and practiced by biblical prophets. For her, as for them, Satan wasn't an aside, a footnote, or a mere teaching tool. He was a force, a being, a creature endlessly trying to tip the scales toward evil. Where bad things happened, like good men getting brain injuries, Satan lurked. Faith in God was the answer. She had sat through countless, passionately delivered Baptist sermons about that very thing.

Plucked from the hundreds of sermons she heard as a child, one specific sentence always struck Brenda as downright ominous: "Without faith, it is impossible to please God."

As a young girl, Brenda thought about those words a lot. Many a summer day, she mulled them over as she trudged around her grandpa's hundred-plus-acre tobacco farm. She chewed on the words as she drifted to sleep at night, the cool sheets warming up under her little legs after she said her prayers in the evening. If she couldn't even begin to please God without faith, well, then it was obvious to her that she better get cracking on it. She felt sure she had never actually experienced faith in her handful of years on this earth. In fact, she didn't think she could precisely say quite what it even was. What was a little girl to do? She had a few ideas.

Gospel messages can easily get lost in translation when traveling from pulpit to pupil, particularly when the pupil is a child. For example, little Brenda sincerely believed that the man named Paul who sat in the back row of the choir most certainly must be the guy from the Bible that the preacher talked about so much. More important, she also believed there were three critical things she absolutely had to do to follow the example of faithful people around her, and she had the distinct impression that each of these things should be done at different times and in a particular order.

The first and most important step was to walk down to the front of the church during "the invitation." This staple of weekly services occurred just after the preacher delivered the sermon. A solid hymn always punctuated his amen as he walked around to the front of the pulpit. There, as the music played, he would issue his invitation to those who had never taken the step to "get saved."

Getting saved meant one thing: personal and public acceptance of God's offer of salvation through Jesus Christ. It was something everybody did at some point in Brenda's church and, as far as she knew, at all churches of like kind everywhere. In the case of children, it meant that a child would, at some point reach the "age of accountability," becoming aware of their sins and their need of a savior. The exact age depended on each individual child, of course, but would be somewhere around the average age of 8 to 10.

Brenda took this step during a series of revival services at her church. "Revivals" were scheduled events that took place two or three times a year. A visiting evangelist would be the featured speaker, and the nightly meetings could last anywhere from a week to three weeks. The revivals would be advertised on signs outside the church, and in the days leading up to them, congregation members would visit homes in the community to invite everybody and their brother to attend. The services consisted of congregational singing, sometimes specially invited guest singing groups, preaching by the evangelist, and the evangelist's invitation at the end of the sermon to come forward to publicly declare any "decisions for God" that had been made by individuals.

These services had an almost electric energy to them, and Brenda felt a strong pull in the pit of her stomach one day to make the brave walk forward. She was nine years old. After she took the visiting evangelist's hand and told him she wanted to get saved, he told her that the pastor would come to her house to talk to her. The words struck fear and dread into her young heart. She had no idea what she should say to him when he showed up on her doorstep, so she worried for days about what to do. The pastor never came.

Little Brenda was terribly confused by this oversight, so at the final revival service, when he invited to come forward all those who had made "professions of faith" during the series, Brenda stayed firmly planted on her rear with her heart pounding. After all, without his dreaded visit to her home, she couldn't be sure if her decision to get saved was legitimate. When the pastor noticed she wasn't getting out of her seat, he called her by name to join the others. She took her spot in a lineup of freshly minted born-again Christians. Though she was relieved, the whole experience temporarily derailed Brenda's three-step plan: she didn't get the courage to walk to the front of the church again for nearly two years.

To her, that second walk down the aisle felt less like a choice and more like a need. It was a need to get baptized, an urge that came on so strong, she could barely wait for the new pastor to finish his sermon. Once he did, wild horses couldn't have stopped her as she marched to the front of the church to get dipped in the divine water that she knew meant eternal life. This was step two for her. The cold water turned warm as it trickled in spindles down and around the curve behind her ears. She felt happy and safe and encouraged as it pooled in her dress collar. On the way home, she overheard her parents wondering to each other why she had waited so long to get baptized.

Just one more step remained now, and it was one she surmised from watching the invitation at each sermon. During almost every invitation, along with those folk who chose to get saved, at least one person would tearfully walk down the aisle to tell the pastor they needed to "re-dedicate their lives." Of great intrigue to Brenda was the whispered conversation that took place between this penitent sinner and the pastor, right before the pastor shared the nature of their decision: to re-dedicate said sinner's life to Christ.

Brenda saw this scene so often, with so many people, that she deduced everyone *needed* to do it. Clearly, it was a salvation booster shoot. When she got around to getting this booster, in her early teens, Brenda felt a great sense of accomplishment. As an adult, she wouldn't remember what specific "sin" was the reason for her decision that day. That's because it wasn't the *why* that mattered so much as the fact that it happened at all. Rededicating herself to Christ completed her spiritual checklist.

All through her growing-up years, Brenda attended Sunday school, Training Union, Girl's Auxiliary (GA), and Bible school—all Baptist organizations and activities. She memorized scripture and participated in Bible drill, a game that teaches children the location of every book in the Bible. Most of her school friends were from Christian families, too. At the rural public school she attended, Bible-reading was done every morning, along with prayer and the Pledge of Allegiance, hands over hearts. Brenda also read her Bible at night before she went to bed because she was taught that all Christians should do so, and she was, by nature, an obedient child. Stretched out on the quilt that covered her bed, she dutifully undertook this quiet time without any particular understanding of the words, convinced that she needed to read at least a chapter each day.

Her first experience with this discipline occurred the summer after she got saved. She was at GA Camp when each girl was given a devotion guide and some designated time and told to find a quiet, secluded spot to sit by herself with God. Brenda found the concept intriguing.

Trying to be alone with God seemed adventurous and unlike her normal family and church life.

Then, in the fifth grade, Brenda's attention turned to a dark-haired boy named Mike Palmer. Mike moved from a nearby community two years earlier and lived less than two miles from Brenda's house with his parents and four younger sisters. He loved to ride his bike on the back-country roads, disappearing for day-long adventures in a time when mothers didn't worry about their children's whereabouts until sundown. Even though he regularly pedaled around the hills that framed Brenda's childhood, even though their community was country and small, and even though he and Brenda rode the same bus sometimes, she didn't notice Mike for nearly two years. After all, they were in different classes, and, more important, Brenda had designs on an older boy.

When she moved up to the seventh grade, the older boy moved on to high school. Brenda and her classmates now changed classes throughout the day, her attention was freed, and she ended up in the same art class with Mike. He was on the short side, by all accounts, but downright handsome to Brenda. He had black hair, dark eyes, and a crooked and sweet little smile that betrayed no wrongdoing. Mike showed an intense talent for math and science, which was different from other kids in their rural community. He wasn't seen as geeky, because he played football and was able to get above-average grades without even studying, but he was sure different. Brenda was intrigued. She got to know him during art class and decided the following year to ask him to a party at her house. Mike showed up for the party in a shirt and tie. Her parents were appropriately impressed, and Brenda fell in love on the spot.

During their fresh-man year of high school, Mike asked Brenda if she would like to "go to-gether."

Of course, going together just meant they were officially a couple. They didn't actually *go* anywhere their parents didn't take them. Brenda's mother and father liked Mike, but they

Brenda and Mike in high school

thought thirteen was a little young to be so serious. They much preferred the idea of their little girl fixating on her schoolwork, which Brenda dutifully continued to do even as she became preoccupied with Mike, who seemed equally preoccupied with her.

Brenda was allowed to invite Mike to her house on Sunday afternoons after church service. And every Sunday, without fail, she began working on that proposition as early as she thought she could get away with it without annoying her parents. It was a delicate balance, but somehow, Mike was always at her house by mid-afternoon to hang out and do whatever her family was doing. He also called her every single night. That's why Brenda loved the sound of the black rotary-dial phone ringing two times from the center of her house.

Back in those days, there were only eight-party telephone lines, which meant that eight families shared the same line. When the phone rang, it rang either once or twice. One-ringers were ignored. Two rings meant the call was for you. At any time, other people who shared the line could pick up their own receivers and listen to any phone conversations taking place by any one of the other eight families. This setup was tricky for lovestruck teenagers hellbent on having their nightly in-depth chat about nothing and everything. Sometimes there was a lot of silence of just being together on the phone.

Mike's dad owned a bulldozer business and was greatly exasperated by the phone situation. His son wasn't the only dating teenager on his family's eight-party line. One day, Mike's dad became so fed up that he called the telephone company and asked for a private line. They told him they could do no such thing that far out in the country.

"Fine," he said. "I want to order eight telephones, and would you please install all of them here at my house?"

He never got those eight phones but instead continued to suffer Mike's and Brenda's nightly phone calls.

Mike was the kind of kid who did everything with an unusual lot of heart and energy. Nothing was ever halfway with him. Brenda sometimes felt sure that if he ever joined the military, he would be the most likely to volunteer for dangerous missions and hurl himself onto live grenades to save his fellow soldiers. The thought, of course, horrified her, so she was grateful he had no such designs. Mike wanted to go to college and was always encouraged in that direction by his dad, who had never finished high school himself.

Mike was a good student and opted to take every math class offered in the school, but his passions were largely divided between Brenda and football. When he was a senior, the local paper did a series of articles on the graduating players. About Mike, the paper wrote: "Mike Palmer, a senior halfback who has played a lot of ball thus far this season, has proven himself to be a valuable cog in the Panther machine. Used primarily as a second-string offensive back early last fall, he has come along at a rapid pace and is now used on both offense and defense. Mike, at 160 pounds, is not one of the big men on this year's squad, but he has made up for lack of size with a fighting heart, which has made him one of the respected members of the Panther team, which has won seven games while losing only one. He has done his part, and you can't ask for more than that."

Mike in football uniform

Brenda admired that fiery spirit in Mike, how intensely he pursued things and his ability to do whatever he put his mind to. *No wonder people get married,* she thought. With God, you could walk down the aisle and stand at the altar and make it known that you were handing your life over to Him. You could partake in ritual acts, holy water poured trickling down your neck, to show that you accepted His saving grace. You could even re-dedicate yourself to Him again and again for a lifetime, whenever the connection seemed tenuous. Without seeing the parallels, Brenda wanted similar things with Mike, though with both situations, she knew that faithfulness was key.

Mike and Stephen on beach in Jupiter, Florida

15

I lay down and slept; I woke again, for the Lord sustained me.
— Psalm 3:5 ESV —

Right away, Mike was processed into the new facility and given a room overlooking the Chesapeake Bay, just as Brenda wanted. This was a good start, but as the minutes turned into hours, and no one came to check on Mike, Brenda grew increasingly distressed. She could not leave without knowing he would be checked on from time to time. Yet, according to the facility's policy, she couldn't stay overnight. Brenda marched her concerns right down to the nurse's station and spoke to the head nurse.

"Mrs. Palmer, you have to realize that this is a rehab facility, not the hospital."

"I'm not sure I follow you."

The nurse gave Brenda a pointed look and a blunt response. "We do not continually check on patients like they do in the hospital. Rehabilitation is designed to force the patient back into reality. Now, we'll come to your husband's room when it's time to prepare him for bed, but as long as there are visitors or family with him, we'll assume he doesn't need us."

This transition was proving to be more traumatic for Brenda than she anticipated. She couldn't really be sure how traumatic it was proving for Mike since he still wasn't communicating well. She needed old Mike to come along and help her and new Mike get things working as they should be. At that moment, she felt alone and overwhelmed with responsibility. It must have shown all over her face, because the nurse softened up a bit as Brenda relayed to her the story of the ambulance accident enroute to the facility.

"I had no idea," the nurse said. "We were all wondering why he was so wet when he arrived."

That night, as Brenda prepared to go home, her heart felt heavy, and her mind was similarly flooded with trepidation. For the first time since the AVM ruptured, Mike was going to be alone overnight. Amanda wouldn't be allowed to hold bedside vigil. Brenda wouldn't be able to get Amanda's updates when she showed up in the morning. It seemed like too much, too soon. Without assistance, Mike was not even able to get out of bed to go to the bathroom. How exactly was this going to work?

Brenda carefully arranged the tray table next to Mike's bed, with a glass of water, a urinal, and a handheld device with the nurse call button on it. She begged Mike to call for help if he needed it, but she had no reason to believe he could understand what she was saying, let alone remember a lick of it. That wasn't her only worry.

Mike's do-it-yourself nature was deeply embedded, and Brenda felt sure that it would trump anything she said. His tendency to figure things out on his own was so much a part of his nature, she was certain he wouldn't push the call button if he needed help. Asking for help was not a Mike thing. Knowing there was little chance the nurses would come to Mike's room without being summoned by him, Brenda struggled mightily with walking away. She tried to leave but managed to turn around and come back several times, pretending she forgot something. Each time, she reminded Mike about the call button and the bedside urinal.

Eventually, she was out of stories and forced her fingers to not touch any more buttons in the elevator other than the one that would take her to the lobby. Then she forced her legs to walk out the front doors and toward the car. She somehow made it across the parking lot, drove home, and spent a long, sleepless night tossing and turning in her bed, filled to bursting with anxiety.

The next morning, she arrived as early as the new rules would allow. She found Mike already up and being prepared for his day by an occupational therapist. Somehow, he had made it through the night alone. Brenda couldn't ask him for the details because he wasn't talking, but now she was more confident that Mike would survive the inpatient portion of his rehab, which his care team loosely anticipated would be a matter of weeks, not months.

The morning was full to bursting with structured activities, therapy after therapy after therapy. Training began from the moment Mike woke, as he was instructed how to dress himself, shave, go to the bathroom, and eat. He had not done any of these activities on his own at the hospital. The whole situation felt very sink-or-swim. Since Mike's right hand and fingers were still somewhat paralyzed, buttoning his shirt proved especially difficult. Tying his shoes was impossible.

When Mike was wheeled into the bathroom, the therapist positioned him in front of the toilet and provided instructions to him and Brenda on how he could go to the bathroom without falling. First, she showed Mike how to manipulate the footrests on the wheelchair so that he could then grab the handrails on one side while Brenda steadied him on the other side. Once Mike was standing, Brenda was told to remind him of the steps involved in manipulating clothing and standing in the correct position. The whole ordeal was broken down into the tiniest of steps, each one necessary to completing the simple task of going to the bathroom.

The family settled into a type of "new normal" schedule, taking turns being with Mike.

Sometimes Brenda and the kids would all be there together, and sometimes they would go alone. Over the coming days, Brenda could see that routine and structure were the foundation of rehabilitation. Each patient in the facility received a daily schedule, which included mealtimes, therapy times, and rest times. Every activity was strictly controlled, and even the most rote tasks, such as holding objects or chewing food, were designed to be part of therapy. Of course, Mike needed them to be just that, since his injury had reduced his skills to a handful of bare-bones functions, including sitting up, taking steps, squeezing an offered hand, chewing food, and making occasional utterances whose meanings could not be discerned. Between strings of therapies, during rest times, Mike would be so spent that he seemed to fall asleep the very second his head hit the pillow. Brenda again was struck by the plain fact that sequence is involved in virtually every task we do. One action follows another in logical, step-by-step order, and the sequence is critically important. It pained her to see the confusion on Mike's face when he was told to brush his teeth. He looked at his toothbrush, the cup, and the water faucet and seemed utterly confounded. As with so many other tasks he would do throughout the day, the therapist intervened, giving him instructions in steps by minuscule steps.

"Pick up the toothpaste," she said. Mike did as he was told. "Open the lid. Good. Now, pick up the toothbrush. Okay, put the toothpaste on the brush. Good. Now, brush your teeth, both the top ones and the bottom ones. Okay, now turn on the water. Next pick up the cup. Okay, place the cup under the faucet. Good. Now fill your mouth with water. Now spit." Many times afterward, Brenda saw Mike place the cup under a dry faucet, forgetting that the water must first be turned on.

Not only was sequencing a challenge but also Mike remained largely paralyzed in his right hand. He could do a bit, but the bit was not much. He didn't even have strength enough to make a fist or anything resembling one. When given something to hold, he weakly curled his fingers around it and stared at it quizzically, as if he wasn't sure how it got there. To help him keep a grip on objects—including his toothbrush and razor—he was given a large handle to attach to them. Because the handle was so large, it was easier for him to hold. He somewhat managed a toothbrush but shaving independently was pie in the sky. Still, the therapist encouraged the family not to despair and pointed out that the goal was self-reliance. To that end, an occupational therapist was present at what they called Meal Club, for the purpose of teaching the patients to feed themselves. Because Mike was not attempting to use his nearly paralyzed right hand, the therapist instructed Brenda to put all of Mike's food and utensils on the right side of the food tray. Doing so was meant to trick the brain into paying attention to the right side, which they felt was key to activating that side of his body. Mike couldn't be fooled. He simply used his left hand to move things back to his left side. Then he would proceed to eat only what was on the left side of his plate.

Ever the researcher, Amanda read of a doctor who was experimenting with forcing use of a patient's weakened limb by pinning down and immobilizing the healthy limb. The restraint literally forced the patient's weakened hand. She and Brenda mentally filed the information away as a possible last-ditch effort should rehab fail to achieve the needed results.

Neina, Mike's speech therapist, was also present at Mike's mealtimes, because part of speech therapy involves the mechanics of swallowing. From a neurological, motor, and sensory standpoint, swallowing and speaking have much in common. They require choreography of many of the same anatomical parts. Paralysis can sometimes cause patients to store food in their mouths without chewing or swallowing. Neina watched to make sure Mike properly chewed and swallowed his food.

The family was also told to watch every bit and monitor the speed of Mike's eating. They vigilantly did so, knowing what a speed-eater Mike had been before his head injury. Many times, Brenda had smirked at him across the dinner table and asked him not to inhale all her hard work. He always smiled back and slowed down his pace. Neina hailed from Pensacola, Florida, an area that is sometimes crudely called the Redneck Riviera. She had a kind face and a smooth, billowing Southern accent that was different from the thick drawls of Brenda's and Mike's home state of rural Tennessee, and different from the rubber-band twangs of the kindly cowpokes in Texas. She was immediately encouraging, gentle, and likable. She also apparently held the keys to a kingdom: by the end of her first formal session with Mike, she had him singing "Happy Birthday."

Brenda was just returning from a meeting with a patient advocate at the time. She had no expectation or sense when she left Mike's side that anything grand would occur in his first session with a speech therapist or she certainly would have stuck around. As she rounded the corner into Mike's room and heard him singing, she was nothing short of astounded. Though Mike's face lacked any hint of emotion as the words dropped from his mouth, Amanda's face looked like that of a parent whose lost child was just returned to her after an abduction. By this time, she already had heard Mike sing the song during Brenda's absence, and she looked so excited to share it with her mom now. Hope! Hope in the abyss! It had been weeks since anyone heard actual words come out of Mike's mouth, and now they were spilling out with ease. How was this even possible?

"People with brain injuries who can't speak often can recite things from memory," Neina explained. "And they can frequently sing even when they're unable to express a sentence otherwise, because of the way the brain stores lyrics and melodies. When we're trying to facilitate turning on the system," she said, "we often start with humming or singing. That's because the right side of the brain can assist the left through melody or emotion." Of course, all of this would take time, and nothing even approaching a conversation could be got from singing a song, but the scene and the conversation proved that Mike still had the mechanical and mental capacity to form whole sentences. For Brenda, that was enough to raise new and much-needed hope. It was almost as if Neina had peeled back the corner of a lid that for weeks seemed irrevocably sealed. The Mike that once was could now be glimpsed again. At least his voice could be heard.

Brenda could not believe what she was hearing. Very few words from Mike in weeks, and now he was singing sentences, and the situation had a funny bent about it. Mike was never one to enjoy singing. In worship services everywhere, there's typically that *one guy* who is standing with his arms folded or his hands in his pockets, lips unmoving while the congregation belts out the hymns. Mike was not quite that guy, but he was close.

Neina didn't stop at just the corner of that lid. From that point on, Brenda looked forward to his sessions with her, knowing that progress likely would be made and that she would be given other tricks to urge along Mike's speech recovery. The not talking was a huge part of the not knowing, and the not knowing was slowly whittling Brenda's resolve. To Brenda, Neina represented hope.

Before Mike's brain bleed, both he and Brenda were prolific conversationalists. They never grew out of their telephone party-line days from high school. They pitied and puzzled over couples in restaurants who barely looked at each other, much less hold a conversation. Never could they imagine being that couple. Brenda shunned the thought even now. Neina helped her to do so. Within days of starting therapy with Neina, Mike was saying actual words. Each one was a salve to Brenda's soul, an encouraging relief to her ears. But in some ways, they also stirred up a new sadness, because they revealed that Mike's voice was changed. It was so soft and slow now that, though it was lacking affect, its quality was almost effeminate. Because a person's voice is so closely associated with his identity, Amanda, in particular, said that she felt her dad was not merely a shadow of his former self, but perhaps another person entirely.

As Mike settled into a routine of daily speech therapy, Neina taught Brenda and their kids a variety of time-tested methods known to stimulate speech. Pivotal to his therapy were flashcards showing common objects—such as animals or people—which Mike was asked to identify by name. If he could not find the word, which was frequently the case, Neina used a series of cues to trigger his memory and help him access it. If she showed him a banana, the cue might be *monkeys eat these* or *these hang in clusters on trees*. All of this cueing was leveled, with some classified as low-level and some as high-level. A mid-level cue might be asking Mike to name the opposite of a word with an obvious opposite, such as *salt*, *hot*, or *day*. And a higher-level cue might be something with far less detail provided, such as *it starts with a B*.

None of these techniques were shots in the dark. Neina carefully selected and introduced them based on Mike's brain imaging and her own observations. First and foremost, it didn't appear Mike had trouble with comprehension, so global aphasia—the most severe type of speech loss, affecting a person's ability to both speak and understand—was ruled out. Rather, the real trouble for Mike continued to be speech-initiation, the ability to *start* talking. To the layperson, Mike could have appeared to be either disinterested in talking or unable to do so again. That was certainly a fear and frustration felt by his family throughout his hospital stay. In reality, the AVM rupture had damaged that supplementary motor area in Mike's brain that serves to *initiate* anything, including speech. He basically needed a new starter. In his case, that new starter would have to be another area of the brain. Neina's work was largely designed to turn on that other area of his brain.

It was a comfort to Brenda that Neina was so certain Mike was not simply refusing to speak. Neina was like the fairy godmother of speech, cracking open little doors and windows in a room where Mike had, figuratively speaking, been trapped in a state of silence. Brenda could see now just how much work it was for Mike to squeeze through those cracks. Neina pointed out that he never refused to try what was asked of him, despite the tiring and frustrating nature of the therapies.

"This struggle is so hard," Neina explained to Brenda. "For some people, it's so hard that they give up. And if they give up, their recovery is not good."

Many individuals with Mike's condition not only give up but also become suicidal because of the extreme isolation they feel. Neina certainly didn't mention this bit of information to the family. Not only might it deflate hope but also it didn't seem quite as relevant in Mike's case: he was on a different trajectory. "Mike has a commitment and a fighting spirit," Neina said. "I can see it. He's a fighter!"

Here was a woman who understood Mike's true nature as a human being, the type of man he was. She understood what Brenda understood, that Mike had an iron will. He did not know how to quit. He did not run from problems. He was the type to go toward a storm when others were running in the opposite direction.

ON AUGUST 27 OF 1979, a tropical storm began to form a few hundred miles off the coast of West Africa and, within days, was upgraded to hurricane status. By the time it hit the Dominican Republic, four days later, Hurricane David was classified a Category 5. As it traveled the Atlantic Ocean, met with the Caribbean Sea, and turned toward the United States, the storm ebbed and flowed, at times appearing to weaken, only to suddenly regain its ferocity again. By the time it turned toward Florida, it was a Category 2 but with a death toll already topping 2,000.

In preparation for Hurricane David, which would go down as one of the deadliest hurricanes of modern times, some 300,000 people evacuated southeastern Florida—where Mike, Brenda, and one-year-old Stephen were living at the time. They weren't part of the mass exodus. Instead, they stayed put, watched the progression of the storm on the news, taking note of what their remaining neighbors were doing. All were out in force, boarding up doors and windows and crisscrossing glass panes with masking tape.

When they first bought their house in Florida, Mike had noticed a stack of oddly shaped pieces of weathered plywood on the back porch. The pieces had little latches all over them. One even had a half-moon shape cut out of it. For the life of him, he couldn't imagine what the wood was for, so he used it to make a few items. He made a simple, squared-off side table for the sunroom and a toy box for the kids. Now, as the winds of Mighty David approached, it dawned on him that the wood was meant for hurricane season—a stock of shutters for the windows and doors. Of the pieces that remained, he discovered that each was perfectly cut for a specific opening on the house. The half-moon was a peephole, for keeping an eye on the storm.

Mike used the remaining wood to board up the intended windows and doors. Then he re-made the plywood covers that were missing. Brenda returned from the store with whatever groceries weren't yet hoarded by others aiming to weather the storm. Having a one-year-old and facing their first hurricane was nerve-wracking, but Mike appeared undaunted. He went about his business of preparing the house just as if it were another of his weekend woodworking projects. In a sense, it *was* his weekend project, for the preparation and the storm itself took place over Labor Day weekend.

When the hurricane arrived, it pounded on their home like an angry mob, its infinite fists of hard rain demanding to be let in. The wind blew so fierce and loud, it sounded like it might suck the paint right off the house. Without ventilation, the air in the house felt warm and thick and stuffy. Brenda marveled at the way Stephen nodded off into his usual nap time during the storm, his cheeks pink and his jagged strands of hair damp with sweat as if he had a fever. Mike was relaxed, and Brenda took her cues from both.

The electricity went out before too long, but Mike had a battery-operated radio, so they were able to listen to the news. After four hours, the voice on the radio told them the eye would be going over soon but that they shouldn't be fooled by the quiet. It would only mean the middle of the storm. Then the winds would blow the other direction for just as long.

"Let's go out," Mike said. "Have a look." When they stepped into their yard, the whole world looked yellow. It was all so quiet, a sort of sleep you didn't know the world could take. For an hour, they stood there in the golden stillness and just marveled. Such unexpected stillness in the center of chaos—trees were felled, and bits of branches and roofing and siding and such were strewn about the streets—but only those who braved the storm would experience that peaceful spectacle.

16

The quickest way for anyone to reach the sun and the light of day is not to run west, chasing after the setting sun, but to head east, plunging into the darkness until one comes to the sunrise.

— Jerry Sittser —

Brenda was consumed with restoring Mike's speech—not just the words but the intonation and, in a way, the soul. It was as though all of the most important answers in the world were locked inside of him now and couldn't be fished out until his speech was awakened. Did he know Brenda? Did he know their kids? Was he afraid? Was he still himself in there? Was he ever coming back to them? She needed the old Mike to stand beside her and help her make sense of this new, strange Mike, to tell her that he was going to be okay. More than anything, she longed to hear him say "I love you" again.

Of course, speech was hardly the only concern. Mike spent many hours a day doing physical therapy. Most of the work was done in a large gymnasium inside the rehab center. It was incredibly bright in the room, and though sunlight poured in through a series of big windows and over several brightly colored therapy balls, the windows did not overlook the Chesapeake Bay like the ones in Mike's room did. They looked out over drab buildings and a once-beautiful neighborhood that was beginning to show its age. When the gym wasn't being used, its ambience was decidedly clinical and cold. Rectangles of fluorescent lights checkered the drop ceiling and cast a bluish sheen on the white linoleum floor. There were a few big, metal U shapes at the edges of the ceiling, and these served as tracks for privacy curtains that could be quickly drawn by the nurses to make an instant "room" if need be. Pegged to the walls or stuffed in wooden shelves were clumps of hula-hoops and all manner of support braces. Big therapy tables held pillows and resistance bands. Dozens of collapsible metal walkers hung together tightly in a long row on one wall. And the centerpiece of everything was a big, wooden, stand-alone staircase that led to and from nowhere. When patients came to the room for therapy, and the hula-hoops and the braces and the walkers and mats came down, the gym came to life. It was full of color and hope.

Mike's daily regimen included getting in and out of a wheelchair, walking, climbing a few stairs on the staircase, reaching with his nearly paralyzed arm, and catching and throwing in any way he could. He was often asked to do one activity with his brain—answer a question, for example—while in an awkward posture, an attempt to make his mind and body work together again. It didn't take long for a strange artifact of his brain damage to make itself known: Mike couldn't drop things with his right hand. It wasn't a physical problem. It was a neurological one. Some part of his brain was preventing him from opening his right fist to release anything in its grip *unless someone else placed their hand directly under the object.* Once something was supporting the object from underneath, Mike could then—open his hand. Things like pitching a ball or throwing a dart would be an impossibility. What's more, he was unable to strike anything with an object held in that hand. He could *almost, almost* make contact, but his swing would stop short. How would he ever golf again if his mind would not let him strike a ball with a golf club? How would he ever be able to enjoy woodworking again if his brain would always want to stop the hammer just short of the nail head?

Physical therapy was so challenging for Mike that he tired very easily and was completely wiped out each afternoon. The old Mike often joked that Brenda was the only one in the family who took naps. If the old Mike ever fell asleep, it was while watching a ballgame, and God forbid anyone should refer to those rare occasions as "naps." Sleeping during the day was *verboten* to Old Mike. Even lying prone in bed was out of the question! Daily afternoon naps were now an inevitability and a welcome reprieve.

Seeing weakness in a man that had always been so strong was a tough pill for the whole family to swallow. Brenda wanted her husband to be the same as he once was in every way, even in things that used to irritate her. She desperately missed seeing his quirky, familiar, annoying habits that made him Mike. She didn't voice this private agony to anyone. Staying positive seemed inextricably tied to keeping the faith.

Helping Brenda keep the faith was that same endless stream of friends that came to her side at the hospital. They came out like stars every night, as everyone finished up their workdays and made their stops to check on Mike's progress. Their faithful attendance kept Brenda's hope for a good outcome alive. If they believed, so could she. And again and again, they told her they believed. Never did any of them discourage her in any way. Not a single person wasted a single word dwelling on Mike's present reality. Brenda received nothing but hope, faith, and love. They brought money, read scripture, and made sure she had creature comforts. Many came to just sit with them, and she found so much solace in their company. Brenda was grateful to Dr. Adam for his advice to choose the rehab facility closest to their home. He was right that the more visitors, the better, realizing that they weren't only good for Mike's rehabilitation; they were essential for her healing, too.

Mike's ability to speak was improving, but the evolution was slow. It could be measured only in hairline, microscopic, tortoise-slow improvements. He still struggled often to find the right word when Neina prompted him in therapy. When he did find the word, he visibly and audibly strained to get it to come up through his body and out of his mouth. It was as if the words were cemented to his insides and had to be pried loose, mammoth-sized things being fished from a deep and narrow well. He still relied mostly on nonverbal communication, and even that was weak and scant.

Because of Mike's inability to say very much, Brenda and the kids still struggled with the gnawing sense that he might not know who they were. They wondered if the nonverbal responses he gave to them when they tried to talk to him, touch him, and connect with him were merely because they had been a fixture at his bedside all those weeks. Perhaps he "knew" them now only because he met them a few weeks earlier and because they sure seemed to hang around a lot, whoever they were. Mike had friends who worked at the shipyards in the distance, and Brenda wondered if he recognized its jagged silhouette for what it was. Did he know there were people across that water that cared deeply about him? Either way, Brenda was convinced of the therapeutic, soothing effects of that view of the Chesapeake. God's wondrous artwork, it sparkled in the sun, dimpled with a thousand tiny whitecaps that kept the scene from becoming a still life. After the rigors of therapy, she made sure he relaxed where he could see it, usually from his room or on the sprawling terrace of the second floor. There, she doggedly watched for signs of the old Mike, tried to provide plenty of stimulation of his memory, and never stopped searching for ways to reacquaint him with his life. She hungered and ached for any trace of the man she knew and loved so much. Daily, hourly, in volumes and iterations that couldn't be measured or counted, she prayed to God for those signs. That faith demands no proof was a reality she accepted about God, but it wasn't one she could so easily swallow about Mike.

Brenda learned from observing Neina that cueing was vitally important to helping Mike speak. He needed the jump-start. "Shut the front..." Neina might say, pausing for Mike to search for the word *door*, unstick it from his insides, and drag it out of his throat. Brenda wondered if she might be able to use cueing to stimulate other memories, too. One afternoon, as she and Mike sat in their usual stillness in the warm sun on the veranda, she turned his wheelchair so that he was facing her. They sat knee-to-knee now, and she started, "Mike, you designed a wind tunnel, and the name of it is *Sky...*"

Without hesitation, Mike answered, "Venture." Brenda could not believe what she was hearing. It was more than she hoped for, such a quick response. She went a step further.

"You built the wind tunnel with Bill..."

"Kitchen," Mike quickly responded.

Brenda excitedly continued by trying as many two-word familiar and specific combinations as she could. He kept going. He responded to each cue without pause, sometimes having to struggle to drag up the word but definitely knowing what word to find. Now she knew. Finally, she knew: Mike was in there. He was with her. He knew exactly who she was and remembered their life. He remembered where it started, and he remembered where it left off.

17

If your God never disagrees with you, you might just be worshiping an idealized version of yourself.
— Tim Keller —

It was July of 1993, and the drive from Alabama to Virginia was over 700 miles, which meant more than eleven hours in the car with a high school freshman and a middle-schooler who could not have been more glum about leaving for new parts. Amanda stewed and sulked in the backseat, one arm draped over Charlie the Spaniel, making it abundantly clear she'd been wronged by the universe and might never recover. Stephen, like his dad, tended to be quietly dignified and choosy about when to speak, so he kept his opinion about the move to himself.

Brenda had never relocated as a child, but Mike had. He could empathize with the kids, but it was unlikely he pitied them. Moving simply

House in Virginia

meant carrying memories from one home to the next. He sometimes shared these with Brenda, who loved to hear about even the bad ones, because of how they shaped him and bound him to another time. Even the bad ones were good, for example when he told her he threw a hatchet at a stump but struck a rubber ball instead, sending the hatchet boomeranging back to clunk him in the forehead (but obviously lived to tell the tale). Another time, he remembered running home to his mother, blood trickling where he'd been shot between the eyes with a BB gun by a neighbor boy. These weren't happy memories, but he seemed fond of them because of the places and people and times to which they tied him. Home was home. Brenda and Mike intended for their daughter's mood to pass.

Amanda's parents had the benefit of retrospect, of course, and they knew there were many good things about moving that Amanda couldn't begin to imagine. They knew that after Mike's childhood memories of riding his bike and playing with his next-door neighbor in one place, there came another school and another house, where a chatty brown-haired girl sat next to him during art class. Then came the memories of holding her hand on long, lazy Sunday afternoons after church let out. Later, came his move to a new town for a co-op job, and with it, the memories of kissing that girl when he returned home to see her on weekends. Yes, Brenda and Mike knew how one move led to another, year by year by year, right up to Al's Steak House, where Mike sat across from that girl, grown into a woman, her brown hair hanging shining and straight to the middle of her back, and gave her an engagement ring. She opened the tiny square box from Meier & Berkele Jewelers and smiled at the biggest diamond Mike could afford, a perfect one-third carat, set in the prettiest setting he could buy. It was the moment that led to the yes that led to the marriage that led to the kids who were now pressing their foreheads, dejectedly, to their respective windows in the backseat of the car.

Not long after they arrived at their new home in Virginia, Brenda noticed Amanda *again* sitting out on a long rope swing that hung from one of the skyscraping oak trees in the backyard. Tears rolled down Amanda's cheeks and plopped onto her shorts. She dragged the toes of her shoes through the dirt and grass as she swung. Brenda knew that Amanda was hoping to be seen there, making a fine show of her misery. However real the sadness, Brenda had finally had enough of it. She marched out to Amanda and told her it was time to shape up lest she be helped to even more distance from the friends she'd left behind—no letters or calls. Amanda's attitude very quickly improved.

In the months to follow, the kids settled in nicely and made new friends as expected.

Then the pages seemed to fly off the calendar for the next few years, both kids busy with school activities, Mike fully entrenched in his job at Micro Craft, and Brenda raising homemaking to an art. She developed and taught "Keepers of the Home," a class at their church for young mothers. It was a course that covered everything from how to organize your home and create a cozy and peaceful environment to marriage and the nurturing and raising of children. Times were good.

Before long, Stephen was graduating and ready to head off to college. They loaded up a pickup truck and drove five hours with him to the campus of Virginia Tech. Back at home, Amanda was busy at her schoolwork, excelling in all her subjects, particularly music. She was speeding so fast that she was due to graduate a full year ahead of time. Mike and Brenda were on the brink of having an empty nest.

Around the time Stephen left for college, Mike was contacted again by Bill Kitchen, the visionary wanting a mobile recreational wind tunnel for the masses. This time, Bill was more aggressive, even insistent. He wanted Mike to pitch the idea to Micro Craft, so he hounded him until he agreed to a personal meeting. Upper management left it to Mike to engage in the meetings with the "nutty guy" after that. They were reluctant to take on something so unfamiliar. Their specialty was handling one-of-a-kind government projects—jobs that posed little to no physical risks to customers. Dabbling in the amusement industry seemed too great a risk, too far outside their lines.

Eventually, Bill became impatient and suggested to Mike that he essentially go renegade and tackle the project on his own. Mike's cohorts were already chatting privately about what it would be like to quit their jobs and tackle such a wild project. Some were excited about the possibility but ultimately didn't dare take the risk. Mike, however, was taking the notion seriously.

Mike at Micro Craft, 10/1995

He had just one caveat: Micro Craft would have to formally reject the project before he would even consider going solo with it. Mike advised Kitchen to request a "put up or shut up" letter from management. They obliged, leaving the door wide open for Mike.

Now Mike and Brenda had a monumental decision to make: gamble or play it safe? Their future was at stake in no small way. Mike had a good, secure job that afforded him a comfortable living. Why leave that behind for something new when they had one son in college and a daughter following soon after?

Brenda once said that Mike "wasn't reckless, but he also wasn't necessarily safe either." His curiosity, confidence, and calculating mind were a recipe for adventure. That's why he rode out the hurricane back in Florida. Mike was simply the sort of man to go toward storms, not run from them. Brenda was never nervous about trusting his lead, however harebrained an idea might seem, because Mike had never failed her. She knew he *had* no harebrained ideas. Rather, all his risk-taking was calculated and carefully weighed. He knew he was capable of just about anything if he put his mind to it, and in Brenda's experience, he was almost always right.

Mike mulled over Bill's proposition for a few weeks. In the end, he decided to negotiate a deal that would make it possible for him to quit his day job—and begin designing the world's first aerodynamically designed recreational wind tunnel. Adventure beckoned.

THERAPY IS NOT FOR THE faint-hearted. Each day in rehab for Mike was filled with intense work, both physical and mental. It started first thing in the morning and usually didn't stop until late afternoon. First, the nurses hung a transparent index cardholder on Mike's wheelchair, containing the scheduled activities and therapies for the day according to time and location. Most sessions lasted an hour, including physical therapy, speech therapy, and occupational therapy.

Also on the schedule were Meal Club, showering, and a daily break. Mike was completely spent by the afternoon, when he finally would be able to nap with the intensity of a feverish child. Yet, after dinner, he would often have visitors in his room or on the terrace.

The family didn't want Mike to go to therapy sessions alone, so almost always he was accompanied by Brenda or Amanda. Occasionally, Stephen would go with him instead. Mostly, Stephen continued being a hero in the background, just as he had during Mike's hospitalization. Stephen was a thinker and doer, not a talker. He owned a forest-green 1995 Mustang GT convertible with great big tires, a 5.0 V-8 engine, and ridiculously loud exhaust system. Loud and showy, it was the antithesis to Stephen, a gentle, quiet, and steadying presence when he came to the rehab center. This was not to be mistaken for passivity.

Brenda knew that when she came home at night, the giant and growing pile of mail on the counter wouldn't be riddled with bills. That's because Stephen would have pulled the bills and tended to them as best he could. He also handled some of the personal correspondence, of which there was plenty. Cards and letters poured in from all over the country, a few from across the ocean even, some from strangers who had heard about Mike through their churches or prayer chains. Brenda was exhausted by the sight of it all, but Stephen took it upon himself to relieve her of that chore as much as possible.

Probably the most voluminous of all was the correspondence from the hospital. It came daily, and other than Brenda's time in labor and delivery, nobody in the Palmer family had ever been hospitalized, certainly not for a month, let alone placed in a rehab facility. This new territory of hospital forms and bills and requests and more forms and more bills and more requests made her head spin. Mike would have been the one to attend to such things in the past. Family finances were his domain. Brenda was too tired to make sense of it all in his stead, so she simply tried to ignore it altogether. Knowing that they had met their $4,000 insurance deductible on the first day of Mike's hospitalization was all she really wanted to know. At least that's what she believed to be true. Stephen seemed to intuitively know that he should step in and, as much as possible, take on the age-old responsibility of "being the man of the family." The fact that he knew to do this—the fact that he knew *how* to do this—lightened Brenda's load tremendously.

As much as Stephen wanted to take care of these things, his hands were often tied: Mike had neglected to get Brenda's name on the business bank account where he kept most of the money. To access the account, she would need a power of attorney but was told she couldn't legally get it without Mike signing off on it. Brenda didn't have a dishonest bone in her body and couldn't even think of forging Mike's signature. Yet he couldn't grip a pen, let alone sign his name! The therapists were working on it and meant business when it came to literally forcing Mike's hand: his right one wouldn't get better if he wasn't forced to use it. In fact, Mike's entire right arm was one of the biggest focuses of daily therapy. He was forced to work it as much as possible, because he tended to ignore it if left to his own devices. To reach any object placed on the right side of his body, he would now reach across his right hand with his left. No matter how menial the task, he did it with his left hand, and with a sloth's swiftness at that.

The clerk at the bank, knowing their situation, advised Brenda to hold off as long as possible to see if Mike might possibly regain the ability to sign his own name instead of going through the hassle of using a power of attorney. So, Brenda and Stephen decided to wait and see, hoping things would change, but the day came when they simply needed the money. With uncertainty, she and Stephen took the document to rehab and explained the situation to Mike. Amazingly, he seemed to understand what they were saying and took the new pen Brenda had given him and signed his own name. His handwriting was tiny and characteristically illegible, but it was his signature.

As often as possible, Brenda wheeled Mike out to the second-story terrace so they could look over the water. One day, as they sat outside chatting with a group of friends, a mosquito landed on Mike's left arm. He responded in small, slow steps. First, he locked his gaze on it, with his head moving ever so slightly to follow it with his lifeless eyes. He still couldn't move his right arm much, so he slowly lifted his left arm up and shooed the mosquito off his arm by blowing on it. Bug bite averted. The entire time, Mike remained quiet and expressionless. He had solved his own problem without anyone really noticing. If ever there were a case to be made for how his therapies were structured—broken down into the tiniest of steps in a very ordered sequence—the mosquito incident was it.

Mike's walking improved at a much faster pace. By June 29, just a week after starting rehab and a month after the AVM rupture, he no longer needed a wheelchair. He walked to each of his therapy sessions now and even went outside the building a few times, but because he was ignoring everything on his right side, he needed close supervision. When he walked the halls of the rehab center, Brenda tried to steer him toward the center of the hallway so he wouldn't knock pictures off the right wall. Outside, the stakes were higher as he faced new obstacles such as gravel and steps. Curbs were especially tricky for him, and any time he tried to negotiate one, he tripped. Watching him walk was equal parts inspiring and unnerving. Meal Club was also unsettling. It took place in a small and spartan room that resembled a board room. It housed a big table and a whiteboard. The patients would bring their trays into the room to eat together and talk with a psychologist. She asked the patients the traditional battery of questions asked when trying to gauge a person's cognition after a brain injury: *Who is the President? What day of the week is it?* And so forth.

Meal Club was one of the few times patients interacted with each other, but to call it *interaction* was a stretch. The patients had a wide variety of head maladies, mostly strokes, that manifested themselves in a number of strange and heartbreaking ways. One of the women spoke exclusively in rhymes. She couldn't help it, but Brenda hated it. She hated hearing it. She hated having a front-row seat to the pain and illness in that room. She already had enough of her own to deal with and didn't need to be so close to everyone else's. Worse, she couldn't help but feel that Mike didn't belong there. She didn't want him in that environment, exposed to the deflating and discouraging sight of so many broken bodies and minds. Mike was the youngest patient, and Brenda was uncomfortable with having him being lumped together with these poor, old souls.

Mike wasn't required to eat at Meal Club, and mostly he didn't. Brenda saw to it that he usually took his meals in his room. They always arrived on a food tray, silverware on the right. He'd cross his body with his left arm to pick up the utensils and then begin the rote task of feeding himself, his eyes vacant and his face slack.

One evening, after she'd gone out to run errands, Brenda returned to the rehab center to find that Mike wasn't in his room. It was past therapy time, past mealtime, past any time when he would need to be out of his bed. Confounded, she went to check with the nurses. "He and your daughter went out for a steak dinner," one said.

Brenda looked at the nurse sideways. Her funny bone was a little rusty, and she wasn't sure she had heard correctly. What kind of joke was this?

"He asked us himself," the nurse continued. "They left about an hour ago." Brenda returned to Mike's room in disbelief. Within the hour, she heard Mike and Amanda coming down the hallway. Both of them were wearing smug, self-satisfied looks—yes, even Mike, who was also sporting a brand new pair of pants.

"Mom," Amanda explained later. "I'm sorry, but I couldn't let him eat what they were feeding him tonight. It was some meat that promised to be a steak but would not deliver. I wanted him to have a real steak."

"What did you do?" Brenda asked.

"I asked him if he wanted to get out of here and get a real steak. I figured we stood a better chance if Dad did the talking, so I told him to tell the nurses at the nurses' station that he wanted to take his daughter out for a steak. We rehearsed the speech a few times, and then I hung back here in the doorway, and he did it."

"Did he now?" Brenda said, showing just a hint of bemusement, of which she had little reserves these days. The whole orchestration was just so Amanda, taking charge and going a little rogue for the greater good. Amanda had always been that way, one of the many ways she took after her dad. That's half of what tickled Brenda. And any accomplishment Mike could

Amanda with her dad, 8/2000

make, in whatever way he could make it, was a victory in Brenda's eyes. "They were definitely reticent," Amanda said. "He kept pointing back at me. You should have seen their faces. They kept talking. They made a call. Then Dad shuffled back here and said we could go, and I took him to Steak & Ale."

"You two." Brenda shook her head. Her wry smile surfaced for a moment.

Her daughter, so strong, and her husband, so determined—she was their greatest admirer. Indeed, Brenda knew Mike was empowered by Amanda's high expectations of him, just as Amanda was once empowered by his high expectations of her. In truth, these weren't expectations so much as faith. Each believed the other capable of extraordinary things, while neither considered their own accomplishments extraordinary. Both were so damned determined, so smart, so industrious.

Brenda could just envision them marching out of that place together in cahoots, no poker faces required. They weren't going to wait for someone else to tell them when to push beyond limits. That was never their way. Why start now?

"He did great, Mom. I had him order for both of us. I coached him how. He rehearsed while I drove, and when it came time, he got it done." Amanda grinned, pleased at this conspiracy to do something normal.

"What about the new pants?" Brenda asked.

"He couldn't walk fast enough to get to the bathroom," Amanda explained. She shrugged. "No big deal. I took him to the mall. The wet ones are in the bag."

Brenda didn't ask how Mike got his old pants off and the new ones on. She didn't ask how Mike covered himself up on the way in and out of the mall. She didn't want to look a gift horse in the mouth, and she was already thinking about what task he might conquer next.

Each physician and therapist who saw Mike continued to bill the insurance company in *a la carte* fashion. The bills were as numbered as the stars, their totals astronomical. When Mike was in the hospital, the family had been assigned a patient advocate, who took care of all conversations with Mike's insurance company, constantly keeping check on what was or wasn't covered during his stay. Periodically, Brenda was assured that the insurance company was agreeing to the continued treatment and hospitalization, as was requested by Mike's doctors.

When it came time to leave the hospital and transition Mike into the rehab facility, Brenda was assured that the rehab would be covered, too. It gave Brenda peace of mind to know that when all of this finally came to an end, there would be no bill to pay on their way out.

About three weeks into Mike's stay in the rehab facility, Brenda was called into the hospital's business office to speak to the patient advocate. She was informed that the insurance policy did not actually cover the rehab bill, only a small portion of it. Brenda knew this was not good news. Sure enough, when she went home and looked over the policy with Stephen, it stated that a rehab facility was covered at the rate of half of the previous hospital's semi-private room rate. Furthermore, other charges were also only partially covered. Brenda called the insurance company to clarify the situation and was informed that the policy was correct: the patient advocate was simply given the wrong information by the insurance company when she originally called to investigate their coverage. So far, the rehab bill totaled $15,000, and if Mike remained at the facility, that number would continue to grow.

Brenda was numb to pretty much everything outside Mike's condition. She didn't have the reserves or capacity to be concerned about little flies in the ointment, and to her, even "big things" like the insurance bill seemed inconsequential in the grand scheme. Paperwork and bureaucracy? Who even cared? Stephen was the only one with the energy for it, so he set about working on the issue as best he could. Brenda continued to focus on Mike's recovery.

MIKE SPENT QUITE A BIT of his rehab time going up and down steps, both inside and outside the facility. Brenda was instructed by the physical therapist to walk backward in front of him as he took each step. He made surprisingly quick progress, which isn't to say it was easy. He seemed to put a great deal of effort into each step. After he conquered steps, his next hurdle was learning how to get in and out of a car.

Again, Brenda was reminded how critical sequencing is in nearly every task of life. Anything we do is built on a series of maneuvers that must be executed in proper order. It was agonizing to watch Mike rediscover the tiny, seemingly simple act of getting into a car. He had to remember to pull the door handle first. Then he must decide which way he was going to fold his body in through the door and onto the seat. He sat down on the seat and then slowly put each leg in. Then he shut the door. The physical therapist had him repeat this process several times over the course of one session. When she was satisfied that he could safely get in and out of the car, she suggested they head back inside. Brenda, however, had other plans.

Brenda appreciated the physical therapist's work, but she felt that none of the therapists knew Mike well enough to ignite something in him. Brenda did, so she was forever looking to find some familiar thing for him to do. Of course, Brenda was painfully aware of how much work it took for him to master the elementary activity of walking outside: negotiating steps, curbs, and gravel, and getting in and out of the car. She just wasn't content to leave it at that, and she suspected she knew what Mike would do now if he were truly still himself.

"Mike," she said offhandedly. "The oil has not been checked in the car since you've been in the hospital."

Mike immediately walked along the side of the car, stepped up on the curb, inched over to the front of the car, pulled the latch on its hood, reached in, pulled out the dipstick, cleaned it off with the rag he kept tucked under the hood, put it back in place, pulled it out again, glanced at it, and then looked over at Brenda and said, "It's fine." Then he replaced the dipstick and started back toward the hospital entrance as if he hadn't just done something extraordinary. The therapist was left staring after him with her jaw dropped. When she looked back at Brenda in astonishment, Brenda just smiled. That, she thought, is Mike.

18

Enter his gates with thanksgiving and his courts with praise!
Give thanks to him; bless his name!
— Psalm 100:4 NIV —

Most mornings, Brenda woke up already exhausted. She had family and friends to buoy her in prayer and in deed, but the old fire inside her now burned on low. Constantly, she watched for God's hands in things and listened in her heart for God's desires for her and Mike. In her prayers, which filled almost every empty space between therapy sessions and conversations, she asked God to show her the way. Sometimes she unleashed her grief in those prayers, resentment percolating over the edges of her sanity. She questioned where the road was leading and then resigned herself to keep walking it, feeling she had no other choice. Surely God would not let her down. On the one hand, she maintained hope. She did not care to hear one word of discouragement, however realistic it might be medically, refusing to think God incapable of giving everything back to Mike—not just *enough* but *everything*. On the other hand, she knew God didn't work on commission.

Brenda continued to believe in what she called "God's perfect knowledge," which meant that He would give her and Mike what they needed. Not only that, but she felt He also knew better than they did what their needs were. Such a tough pill to swallow: the thought that God somehow felt she or Mike "needed" what was happening to them.

Brenda revisited Bible stories that revealed the most excruciating handiwork of God, how harsh He could seem. She was familiar with Job's story—his livestock and livelihood destroyed, his servants murdered, his ten children crushed to death as their home collapsed under a mighty wind. Job's faith and trust in God was greatly tested by a string of tragedies, but he displayed an abundance of faith. Brenda refused to believe that she or Mike were being punished by God for anything. She did not believe God was the author of evil, pain, and suffering in their lives. Yet she found herself struggling to understand, in practice, what she had so long accepted in theory about His mysterious nature: God doesn't always answer our prayers when or how we want.

Maybe it would all make sense later? Wondering where they were heading was inevitable—knowing that God's work does not follow any earthly blueprint—and the waiting was like a slow drip boring a hole in her spirit. When she allowed her mind to wander toward the *what if 's* and the *why me's*, Brenda told herself it was the devil's handiwork, doubt and distrust slithering into unguarded areas of her heart. She reminded herself repeatedly to trust in the Lord. Though the doing was hard, the seeds of this faith had been deeply planted more than forty years earlier and nurtured every day of her life. Their blossoms proved still alive each day, if somewhat wilted.

When she consciously worked to find glimmers of hope in the progress Mike was making, she saw there were many! She found ways to smile and appreciate small steps toward his full restoration. But as she drove home in the evenings or awoke in the mornings, she did not look out the windows and marvel at the beauty of God's creation so easily anymore. She noticed the bent branches, the muddied streams, the dirty haze over the shipyards, the way the sun cracked open the pavement and dried up the grass. She felt cracked open, too, even as—or especially as—the real possibility of Mike's homecoming came into focus.

As much as Brenda looked forward to having Mike home, she knew deep down that "magical thinking" was at play: she subconsciously equated his return with his full restoration. It was foolish to imagine that having him home could somehow erase the mess of the past month and a half. She knew better. She knew it was denial. Yet when she allowed herself to face the reality of the situation, she was too overwhelmed. She could not imagine what their marriage or home life would be like if Mike continued to be this shadow of his former self, like a stranger in her husband's skin.

Every therapy was designed to restore all that Mike had lost, but she now understood that graduation from rehab would not be equivalent to full restoration. To be discharged, Mike simply had to be able to function well enough to be relatively safe away from the facility. Of course, speech and physical therapies would continue when he left, but the burden of round-the-clock care would shift onto Brenda's shoulders. Eventually, the kids would return to their lives, and that thought overwhelmed her. Would the old Mike be back in weeks? in months? in years? Would that person be back at all?

It started with baby steps: within days of the incident with the oil check, Mike was given the okay by his doctor to come home for a single daytime visit. Brenda and the kids were to pick him up on a Saturday morning, July 1, and return him to the rehab center by five o'clock that evening. They were told to bring him back earlier if things became too difficult for him. If this first visit went well, they could do the same the following day.

It was hard for Brenda to believe that only about six weeks had passed since the AVM rupture. Only two or three weeks had passed in rehab. When almost every minute hurts and is a drain on the body and spirit, time moves with cinder blocks around its ankles.

On the morning of Mike's home visit, Brenda stayed home to fix a big breakfast for the family, something she used to do all the time. It lifted her spirit a little and helped her prepare for the day ahead. Stephen and Amanda picked up Mike in Stephen's Mustang convertible and drove him home on the serpentine roads with the wind blowing around them and enveloping them in a protective layer of white noise. In the trunk of the car was the wheelchair the rehab center had required them to take. The whole family had an unspoken understanding that the trunk was exactly where that chair would stay. When they arrived at the house, Brenda met them at the car, putting on her best smile.

Then the family walked together up the brick pathway to the front door. It was a slow but steady plod, Mike's new pace, but nobody wanted to race ahead of him. As soon as he crossed the threshold, Mike broke away from the pack a little and headed straight back to his office. Brenda followed him and watched as he sat down in the big, executive office chair where she had found him that awful morning six weeks earlier. Immediately after he sat down, tears began to flow down his cheeks. He had finally come full circle. Brenda walked away and let him have some time to himself while she finished putting breakfast on the table.

They kept the rest of the day simple by doing everyday things like playing billiards and Monopoly, walking around the yard, going into Mike's woodshop in the backyard, watching TV, and taking a nap. Mike oversaw Amanda changing the oil in her car. Later in the afternoon, they sat together, talking and trying their hardest to act naturally. At one point, they tried to discuss taxes and business, but Mike became visibly upset. Though unable to put into words what he was feeling, it was clear from his furrowed brow and sighing and from the way he lifted and lowered his left hand as if to say something and then resigned himself to being unable, that the conversation should be set aside.

A few visitors came by that day, including their next-door neighbor, Buddy, and his son, Joe. They stayed just a short time, but it was significant. Mike seemed pleased to see them. There was the slightest light in his usually flat expression. The visit might have looked uncomfortable to an outsider. Indeed, it might have been uncomfortable for Buddy and Joe, but they didn't betray that discomfort to Mike. Sitting together without a steady flow of conversation, without any real reciprocation of words, was the new normal. People talked *at* Mike, not *with* him, but they did so with great gentleness and patience, and Mike responded mostly by nodding or holding their gaze.

"Mike, never give up," Joe said.

Brenda thought how important those words were. Someone other than family was acknowledging to Mike that he was in a fight, and that he could see him working at it and believed he could prevail.

Later that day came Stan and Joe and Robin, who were some of Mike and Brenda's closest friends. It was so good to be home with people that they cared about so much, just stopping by like old times. It wasn't quite normal, but it was a hint of it.

When the time came for Mike to leave, Brenda walked with him slowly to the car. The kids stayed behind after hugging their dad and telling him they loved him and would see him the next day. Brenda could see in his face that he wished he could stay. She wished he could, too.

The final week in the rehab center was spent working with the physical therapist more on negotiating stairs, walking outside, and even—to Brenda's astonishment—jogging down the hallway. Mike accomplished this feat without any real problems. He was even taken to the outpatient building that was adjacent to the rehab center so that he could walk on a treadmill. He managed to stay on the moving belt without tripping or falling off.

He was still far from any semblance of his former self, though. In addition to his flat affect, even as his body was gaining strength, his affect was flat and his voice betrayed weakness and emptiness. It held no volume. It didn't carry. It was not the voice of a strong man and sometimes seemed effeminate. Amanda was particularly troubled by this. Her frustration and sadness finally boiled over one afternoon, when Mike spoke her name like a child would. She could barely hear or understand him. Missing her strong daddy, she stiffened up her spine and announced she had had enough.

"This is not your voice," she said firmly. "I can't hear you. You don't talk that way. I'm leaving here right now, and if you want me to return, then you better call my name. If I can't hear you, I won't be coming back."

As she walked away, Mike initially started calling out with the same slow, weak, and mousy little *Amanda*. It must have been excruciating for her, but she stuck to her guns and kept walking away with confidence, not evening turning back to remind him of her demands. He made a couple of feeble attempts before finally managing to call out her name with both volume and oomph. "AMANDA!" he yelled. She immediately came back to him.

Much of the work of getting Mike back was just like that: reminding him of who he was, how he talked, walked, looked, reacted, responded, felt—what he was even supposed to care about. Amanda's experiment and others like Brenda calling him on the phone to coax words out of him, helped all of them know he deeply wanted to please the ones he loved. This proved to be useful information. Brenda, Amanda, and Stephen were willing to use whatever it took to push, prod, encourage or even manipulate him back into his old self.

Brain injury is a losing of personality, inner drives, and motivations; a distancing of what makes a person who they are. Brenda knew Mike better than anyone and she could see that part of her new role as his wife was to remind him and even tell him just who Mike Palmer had been and was going to become again. She knew it would be a long-distance marathon. Reminders would need to be repeated over and over, but she was determined to do whatever it took, because the stakes were high and failure was out of the question. *Mike, this is who you are. This is what you do. That is how you do that.*

And then it happened. Dr. Ross pronounced Mike ready for release. It was finally time to go home. Coming home permanently was a welcome milestone in the journey. Brenda realized that even in her weeks of trepidations about caring for Mike alone, she never truly allowed herself to imagine that he was coming home to her.

On the Friday morning when he was to be released, she brought a shirt and tie for him to wear. He walked down the hallway looking more like one of the staff doctors than like a patient who had been wheeled in on a rain-soaked gurney just a few weeks earlier. It was the seventh of July, 45 days since they had begun this journey.

IN MANY WAYS, IT WAS wonderful to have Mike home, but in other ways, Brenda found it just plain awful. Having to face their reality square in the face, day in and day out, amplified the emotional pain. It was helpful to have Stephen and Amanda home with them, but it was also strange and different, because Brenda and Mike had grown accustomed to their empty nest. Now they were all together again under the most stressful and sorrowful circumstances.

Brenda was sleeping next to a man she knew yet hardly recognized anymore. He even slept in a completely different position—flat and stiff on his back instead of relaxed on his side. And for a while, Brenda barely slept at all. Mike now got up to go to the bathroom in the middle of the night, something he seldom did, and Brenda lived in constant fear that he would trip over the steps going up to the bathroom and injure himself. She held her breath every single time he got out of bed, and no matter how many times she pleaded with him to turn on the light, he just wouldn't comply. Even though he needed to add such practical routines, he simply defaulted to his old habits, refusing to make allowances for his deficits. The fact that he remembered himself, his old habits, was good. Yet not adjusting added stress to the situation for Brenda.

Now that she had him home at night, Brenda wanted to talk to Mike. She wanted him to talk to her. Their old nights of pillow-talk were painfully missing, but Mike at least seemed more relaxed and like his old self when he lay in bed next to her. It was at that time each night that she missed him most, because normally, in their past, there would have been conversation. Now, she could not help but talk and talk incessantly, telling him everything that happened during that day as well as over the previous weeks, again and again. He put up with anything and everything she said and did, unable to stop or limit her need to talk, no matter how long the hours drew out. She knew that this late-night talking wasn't good for either one of them, but she couldn't help herself. It was an itch she had to scratch.

One evening, after they went to bed and Brenda was blessedly done talking, things got quiet and Mike suddenly sprung out of bed, turned on the light, went downstairs, and came back with a screwdriver. Brenda lay in bed, hardly breathing and in absolute astonishment as he turned off the ceiling fan, managed to climb up on a trunk at the foot of the bed, and started working on the fan with the screwdriver. When he accomplished what he meant to do—stop a clicking noise—he climbed back down off the trunk, put the screwdriver down, turned the fan on, turned off the light and got back into bed, never saying a word. Brenda was bewildered and shocked at seeing him take action this way, but it was classic Mike. She lay there quietly with her heart pounding, listening to the now-smooth and regular rotation of the wooden blades overhead as they pushed cool air down upon her face. She was afraid to say anything for fear that he would claim that he didn't know what on earth she was talking about. So, without words, she thanked God from the depths of her soul for what she had just witnessed.

ON THE FIRST SUNDAY MORNING after Mike's homecoming, trying to feel normal and get back into familiar routines, Brenda reluctantly asked Mike if he wanted to go to church.

Honestly, she didn't want to go and assumed he wouldn't be ready. Amid everything they were doing—having him home, trying to figure out what that meant, feeling the heavy responsibility for their whole household and future—going to a public place with so many people did not appeal to her in any way. But when she asked Mike, he assured her that he *did* want to go. In spite of her reticence, she recognized his response as the signature curiosity of the "old" Mike.

As they drove into the massive parking lot that surrounded the domed mega-church, Brenda wondered if they had made a mistake. Everything in her wanted to turn around and go back home, shut the door, keeping the outside world at bay for as long as possible. She kept her misgivings to herself as they walked toward the sound of exuberant singing wafting through the numerous sets of double glass doors that led into the circular lobby. As they approached the bottom of the steps, they recognized a man named Lawrence, who rushed to them, obviously excited to see them there. They had met him at Riverside Hospital. Lawrence showed up to Mike's room one day in his scrubs, explaining that he was a member of their church and had heard about Mike's situation when Ron had asked the church to pray for him. Over the course of Mike's time in the hospital, Lawrence had dropped by his room several times, eager to encourage and pray with him.

As they greeted him, Lawrence seemed to sense Brenda's reluctance to face the large crowd. He said, "These people need to see Mike. They have been praying for him—a lot! Seeing him walk through those doors, doing so well again, will boost their faith and encourage them in their own lives. This is not just about you. This is about them too!" Those words gave Brenda the reason she needed to keep going.

As they entered from the rear doors of the enormous circular sanctuary, they slipped into the end of the back row bench, hidden underneath an angular overhung balcony. It felt comforting, but it was awkward to be back in this familiar place. The sound of the mingled voices seemed louder and the place more expansive and intimidating than they remembered.

When the singing stopped, Ron approached the acrylic podium and asked the congregation to take their seats. "I will not ask him to speak, but I am so pleased to see that Mike Palmer has entered the back of the room. Mike, please stand so everyone can see you."

Completely taken by surprise and unprepared for what was about to happen, Mike slowly rose to his feet. A massive wave of applause filled the auditorium as hundreds of people turned to look at him standing, alive, breathing and looking, as far as they could tell, completely normal and healthy. It was one thing to hear that people were supporting him and praying for him—it was quite another to witness this display of heartfelt joy and thankfulness at his recovery. Brenda knew it was right for them to be there and that Mike needed to see this. They both did.

Mike at Sky Venture construction site
in Orlando, Florida, 2/1998

First flyer in SkyVenture tunnel, 6/1998

19

Oh, Lord GOD! You have made the heavens and earth by
Your great power and outstretched arm. Nothing is too difficult for You!
— Jeremiah 32:17 *NASB* —

The year was 1998. Finally, construction of Mike's design was ready to begin. A recreational skydiving wind tunnel of this type had never been tested, and Mike and Brenda were filled with a mix of uncertainty and excitement at the prospect of launching into this unknown territory.

After being fabricated, the various components for the tunnel were loaded onto ten shipping containers headed to Orlando, Florida, where they would be assembled just off International Drive close to Universal Studios. A steel erection company was hired, and the construction manager began site preparation, supervising the early stages of the steel erection.

Upon arriving in Orlando, Mike and Brenda drove directly to the site. It was early evening, and all the workers had gone home for the day. What a feeling it was to be standing there together, husband and wife, looking at something Mike had designed becoming so *real*.

That night, they situated themselves in Bill's garage apartment in Celebration, Florida, a Mayberry-like town built by Disney. Celebration was perfection through and through, reminiscent of *The Truman Show*. Mike was off to an early start on Monday morning as Brenda settled into the tiny apartment. This was to be their home away from home for the next six months as the tunnel was being built.

Mike completely immersed himself in the everyday decisions and challenges of building something brand new. He had been around some type of construction all his life, but this was something considerably more challenging and with much higher stakes.

Little by little, the tunnel began to take shape. It was an oddly configured structure, and by mid-spring, curious onlookers along International Drive were asking the obvious: "What is it?"

Mike's anxiousness intensified as completion of the project drew near. One evening, as startup day was approaching, he and Brenda were standing in the small apartment staring out the window when Mike casually said, "I sure hope this thing works." Brenda could not believe her ears. Even though she had been privately voicing anxious prayers, she had never heard *Mike* question whether it was going to work. She looked up at him and screamed, "Are you kidding me!? What do you mean it might not work!? Is that a possibility!?"

"It works on paper," he replied. "I think it's going to work, but I'm not absolutely positive." Mike sensed her sudden fear and tried to reassure her. However, the seed of doubt had been planted in her mind, and from then on, her anxiety rose while her prayers became more desperate and frantic.

As work progressed, Bill began hiring the personnel that would be needed to manage and oversee the running of the tunnel. He was also searching for instructors who had specific experience skydiving. He found possibilities from among the young skydivers who were working for a skydiving operation called Flyaway in Pigeon Forge, Tennessee.

Finally, the day arrived when it was time to start up the tunnel. That morning, Mike departed to the building site and promised to call Brenda when it came time to throw the switch for the first time. She spent the morning praying and anxiously waiting. When the call finally came, they had already started it up for the first time, finding that it wasn't producing enough wind. Mike had quickly discovered the reason and re-pitched the blades. When they next cranked up the motors, it worked. One of the newly arrived, experienced skydiving instructors was the first to fly. He was able to successfully fly dressed only in shorts, with no shirt, needing no flight suit—a testament to the smoothness of the airflow. When Mike called to give Brenda the good news, she jumped in the car and quickly made her way to the site in record time. When she arrived at the tunnel, she saw a look of great relief and joy on Mike's face.

Bill happened to be out of town on that morning. For only a short period of time, construction came to a halt as many of the believers and skeptics watched Mike make a call to him. "Bill, it works! We are flying our first person at 125 mph!"

Mike was tired, sweaty, and dirty but inexpressibly happy. Champagne was sipped in paper cups and work was quickly resumed, as the need to start generating revenue became the next order of business.

Over the next few weeks, the tunnel site was abuzz with the activity of plumbers, electricians, painters, HVAC contractors, carpenters and landscapers. As with most construction projects, the last details seemed to take the most time, with completion continuously just out of sight. This project was no different, and tempers sometimes grew short. Because this was a bare-bones prototype, the construction trailer was turned into a temporary sales office, and Bill asked Brenda to oversee getting it cleaned up and ready to open for business. She was glad to be included. It felt good to be contributing to what Mike was doing. A soft opening was finally held on July 14, 1998. The mood was upbeat, but everyone involved, especially Mike and Bill, knew that the next several days and weeks were going to be critical to future sales and the project's long-term success. The structure itself was quite a sight, visible to tourists approaching Universal Studios from I-4. Curious onlookers continuously stopped to ask what in the world it was. There were a variety of guesses, but tourists weren't sure what to make of it since they had never seen anything like it.

The tunnel was open for business daily between 4 p.m. and midnight, catering to tourists who spent the day at the theme parks and were seeking entertainment among the busy and alluring attractions along International Drive. Mike felt a deep sense of satisfaction.

At the same time, Mike knew the verdict on operating and running the tunnel was still out. As he and Brenda finally packed their car for the return trip home, his mind was already onto the next steps. Once they arrived, he lost no time getting to work correcting drawings while answering the phone calls that now came hourly from those operating the tunnel. The running of the tunnel was unfamiliar, and there were continual questions about how and what to do as various technical issues arose.

151

In addition to amusement customers and sky diving enthusiasts, some military personnel began to take an interest in the new tunnel. Bill continued to work out the kinks of the operation, while Mike spent long hours changing and correcting drawings and working on a potential design for a second facility in California. He had daily conversations with Bill about potential customers and methods to sell the new idea. The tunnel continued to work magnificently, and over the next year and a half, word about it had spread throughout the skydiving world. The statistics were good, and multiple sales seemed right around the corner. In January of 2000, Mike was invited to deliver a technical paper, "Affordable Air," at the American Institute of Aeronautics and Astronautics Ground Test conference in Reno, Nevada. Mike's design and the operation of SkyVenture was proving that producing smooth, 125 mph winds (the terminal velocity of skydiving) in an indoor skydiving wind tunnel was both possible and affordable. Fellow engineers and students who heard Mike deliver his speech that day could not have guessed that four months later, he wouldn't be able to say a single word, differentiate a penny from a dime, or go to the bathroom on his own.

20

Within days of Mike's coming home from the rehab facility, Bill Kitchen called to say he wanted to come again for a visit. Brenda was unnerved by the prospect, but she knew that there was a need to discuss Mike's future involvement in SkyVenture and their financial needs as they faced the long stretch of recovery ahead. The situation was still raw and overwhelming, but Brenda agreed to his visit because she felt she had no choice.

At the same time, Mike's parents were traveling home to Tennessee from a trip and called to let Brenda know they were coming to visit enroute. Brenda was dazed and exhausted with just having Mike home and anxious about Bill's visit. Family visitors would be too much.

Brenda loved Mike's parents as if they were her own and knew they were hurting, but she didn't know how to comfort them and instinctively wouldn't allow them to penetrate the small, insular bubble she kept around herself to stay buoyed. Their anguish felt almost like an omen, a sign of hopelessness and doubt. As a mother, she understood that they were experiencing heartbreak, but she couldn't tap into that empathy just yet. Blinded by her own pain, she was running on emotional fumes.

Mike was upstairs during the call from his dad, but he evidently overheard Brenda's side of the conversation. She asked his dad to please postpone their visit for a few days and allow her to get past Bill's visit. He was understandably anxious to see Mike for himself and felt pushed away and unwelcome. Brenda was sad about the exchange but didn't know what else to do. As soon as she hung up, she walked upstairs and found Mike standing in the middle of their bedroom looking distressed. He came to Brenda, put his arms around her, and said very clearly, "I'm sorry about all of this."

Brenda was thrilled, not because he might have been siding with her but because he seemed in that moment to grasp the burden she was carrying. It was also the most words he had independently strung together since his AVM rupture. With them, he was supporting her as much as he was able. It allowed Brenda to glimpse the true nature of his perception at the time, of his awareness of the details that dictate relationships. Brenda hated the momentary rift with his parents but was filled with gratitude for this unexpected visit from the old Mike. It showed an important change in his outward condition, one that told her something significant about his inward condition. He was aware of more than he could show.

THE DAY BILL ARRIVED, BRENDA and Mike went to pick him up at the private airport near their home. When he walked into the terminal, his face betrayed no sign of surprise. He did not acknowledge the enormous change in Mike's condition from just weeks earlier in the ICU. He simply acted as if Mike were exactly as he expected him to be—exactly as he'd always been. During the drive back to the house, Brenda took her cues from Bill and chatted as if nothing at all had happened. Mike didn't make a peep. Even though he was occasionally able to string together a few words in a coherent way, conducting conversation was pie in the sky.

At the house, the three of them sat together, and Brenda and Bill eked out some small talk. Brenda was grateful to Bill for keeping the conversation light. He told Mike to get well. He assured him that he wanted him to devote himself to doing what it took to recover. Then he set up a modest consulting fee schedule and said he would need information and expertise from Mike as they moved forward with pursuing sales of the SkyVenture wind tunnels.

During most of the meeting, Mike was stone silent, though Bill asked him a couple of specific questions concerning the tunnel. Brenda suspected

Bill was merely fishing for clues about Mike's awareness and memory. One of the questions he asked was whether the fan-guards at the bottom of the fans could hold the weight of a man standing on them to do repair work.

Brenda was pleased to watch as Mike answered the question with a decisive and confident YES, not hesitating for even a moment. This quick response was another indication to Brenda that Mike knew and remembered details of his work. His answer seemed to satisfy Bill, so they wrapped up the serious talk and headed out for dinner before taking Bill back to the airport. It was a short visit, but Brenda felt that it was a significant step. Bill's visit lifted some of the worry about money, at least as a stopgap. Things had been tight before the AVM rupture because Mike was no longer employed at a day job, instead investing and risking his time on SkyVenture. He took that risk because he was confident in the project, never really doubting that gratification in the form of dollars would come. The consulting fee that Bill was offering now wasn't much, but it did allow Mike and Brenda the freedom to concentrate more of their energy on Mike's recovery.

When Mike's parents arrived a few days later, the visit was the same as many of their previous visits to Virginia. They talked and acted as if nothing had happened. They shared meals as a family and then drove around in the car, a good way to pass the time together. His mom and dad made few references to his illness unless Brenda or Mike brought it up. To her, they appeared somewhat uncomfortable with the fact that he was struggling to get words out, so they just talked for him, filling in every word they possibly could. It was surely painful for them to watch Mike struggle to speak; this was their much-loved son. Brenda thought that they were handling that pain but not calling attention to the obvious deficits. It was soon time for them to leave, and as they drove away, Brenda was once again alone with the burden of moving on.

Their days were now filled with outpatient therapies—reading aloud, fine-motor activities, games, singing, walking. Brenda did all she could imagine might bring renewal to Mike's brain, body or both. Amanda worked with him specifically on reading and math.

Watching daughter start off dad with simple addition was almost too painful for Brenda to bear. Mike was the engineer, and she was the little girl who admired him. Math is the mainstay for any engineer, and Brenda didn't know what they were going to do if he was unable to do it. She wondered if he might need to go back to school but didn't know if he could.

One of the problems that can surface for people with brain injury is the inability to learn new things. Mike didn't seem to be in that unfortunate group. Under Amanda's tutelage, he actually seemed to move quickly from one level to the next. With each problem, he needed only initial reminding on how it was done. Math was like an old friend, its face changed just enough that Mike needed to be reminded he knew it.

Reading was another story: a distant stranger. Mike struggled mightily with it now.

Reading difficulties are common among brain-injury patients and can wreak havoc on their lives. For many people, being unable to read means lasting unemployment. Brenda and the kids started off by having Mike read the simplest things they could find. The going was painfully slow, and Mike continually made up words as he went, so someone always sat with him to provide the corrections. Often, his eyes would catch the words both above and below the line he was reading, and the result would be a garbled string of nonsense. A therapist advised them to use a straightedge, such as a ruler, to help resolve this problem, but this crutch seemed to irritate Mike. He never needed one for reading in the past, so he certainly didn't want one now.

Brenda was grateful for the times that the kids worked with Mike. She also was grateful when Neina, the speech therapist, came for their appointments and took the reins. She desperately needed these breaks from watching her husband struggle, hour after hour, day after day. She was forever comparing his current condition to his past abilities. In her children's faces, she saw a reflection of this same pain and desperation. Neina had quickly became fond of the family during Mike's stay in rehab and was personally intrigued from a professional standpoint, by both his age and occupation. He was relatively young for his condition, and his vocation was complex and demanding of high intelligence. Perhaps because of this personal interest, she offered to see Mike privately after he was discharged to live at home again. He had an obvious rapport with her and needed as much help as he could get with his speech. Neina began visiting the house on a weekly basis.

Her visits weren't free, and eventually Brenda and Mike realized that the cost was prohibitive, so Neina came up with a workaround: she put in a recommendation for Mike to Dr. Stacie Raymer, a professor in the speech department at Old Dominion University in Norfolk. She hoped he would be a possible candidate for a study Dr. Raymer was conducting with the help of her students.

Dr. Raymer had been Neina's professor at Old Dominion and, based on their relationship and her trust of Neina's recommendation, Dr. Raymer agreed to work with Mike. As a study participant, Mike was ordered to get a new brain scan. After meeting this requirement, the Palmers began making the 30-minute drive to the university three times a week.

In the waiting area during visits, Brenda and Mike found themselves among much older couples. Brenda couldn't help but notice that, in most cases, it was the husband who needed the therapy. This was typically due to stroke. All these men wore braces on their hands, legs, or both to support their weakened muscles. They seemed to be several years into their ailments, and Brenda looked on them with a sense of trepidation and fear. She hoped she wasn't looking at Mike's future. Mike's involvement in the study afforded him the chance to receive additional speech therapy from graduate students in the speech-language department of the university. They worked with him through a variety of activities, including naming objects, explaining processes, describing pictures, and engaging in casual conversation with students. Of course, it sounded anything but casual at Mike's cadence and with his stuttered starts, but it was progress.

Brenda always accompanied Mike to these visits and, very often, she sat with Dr. Raymer outside the tiny therapy rooms, observing the sessions through a two-way mirror. It was a strange feeling, to observe him like the specimen that he was to these people. However benevolent their motivations might be, Mike was still a case study. The students usually asked Mike to perform simple tasks such as writing his ABCs in alphabetical order, and the simplicity of these assignments—how they visibly challenged Mike— left Brenda with a pain in the pit of her stomach. She suppressed an urge to scream answers to him through the glass as these young college students sometimes treated him like a child.

Of course, they didn't know who Mike was. They didn't know what brilliance he possessed, the genius that was buried underneath the injury, waiting to be released from the rubble that kept him trapped. They were obviously interested in helping him, but Brenda could not help but think that they simply didn't know who they were dealing with. She was desperate to explain who he was and the exceptional kind of mind and spirit he possessed. Mike was their artistic medium, and they didn't even know what glorious things were waiting to be shaped in their hands! Physically, Mike was still quite weak. Though he never used a walker, cane, or wheelchair and could even jog a tiny bit, he generally moved at a sloth's pace. But he also had a good friend waiting in the wings to help with this piece of his recovery, Kevin Parrott.

Kevin is the friend who was to play golf with Mike the morning of the AVM rupture, and he was a big believer in prayer. He regularly visited Mike in the hospital—even helping him in and out of his hospital bed a few times—and watched his progress with great interest and encouragement. Even in those first uncertain weeks of recovery, he insisted he was going to work with Mike in the gym as soon as he was home and had permission from his doctor.

Mike with Kevin Parrott

When that day arrived, Brenda drove Mike to the gym and watched Kevin weigh him and take his measurements. Mike had thinned and lost a lot of weight. Brenda found it difficult to have Mike's weakness quantified in this way, and she realized very quickly that she didn't have it in her to stay and watch him endure whatever therapies Kevin was going to dole out. She knew Kevin knew what he was doing and could be trusted, but she also suspected he would challenge Mike to his very limits, just as Mike probably would want. It wouldn't be pretty.

Though Mike was walking by this time, he still easily tripped over any unevenness in his path and somewhat dragged his right leg. His right arm hung limply at his side, and he continued to ignore the weakened side of his body, as if it were a stowaway he was burdened to haul with him everywhere. Even the simplest manual tasks he tackled with his left hand, despite being right-handed his whole life. Kevin's workout plan took all these deficits into account and were tailored to address them as quickly as possible. By now, Brenda was accustomed to her new role as Mike's protector, though it represented a complete role-reversal in their marriage. Even so, she couldn't protect him from Kevin, who sometimes seemed almost ruthless when he put on his personal-training hat. She completely trusted Kevin and felt she could dial down her mother-hen impulses when he was with Mike. Yet she decided early on that it would be best for everyone if she used their workout times to recharge herself.

Kevin told her about a manmade lake with a fountain just down the road from the gym. It was a quiet and secluded place, a refuge where she could read and collect her thoughts. Brenda spent many hours at this lake, not only reading but also walking the perimeter and wondering why the complex was even there: it had so few visitors. The place was the future home of a new city hall and shopping area, but she knew nothing of it, and she sometimes pretended it was placed there just for her: Somebody had spent a lot of money building a beautiful lake surrounded by sidewalks, trees, and benches just for this moment in her life! Brenda liked to imagine that they had started with the lake and fountain so she would have a place to rest while Mike worked. Sometimes it helped.

Mike settled into a routine of twice-weekly personal workouts with Kevin. One of the days was spent working exclusively on Mike's upper body. The other was spent on his lower body, combined with some sort of cardiovascular activity such as the treadmill, stationary bike, or elliptical machine. Mike's strength and coordination improved quickly, and within weeks, his muscles began to tone up. In some ways, his body looked even better than it had before the AVM rupture. "What is the value of a man's physical strength?" Brenda wrote in a letter to Kevin one afternoon. "What is the value of a man's agility and coordination? There's no way to place a value on what you've given Mike. He is many orders of magnitude better today because you have given what you've given."

After Mike's first few weeks out of rehab, Brenda again was informed that their insurance policy wasn't sufficient; it didn't cover Mike's many home therapies or the outpatient speech therapy he needed and had been receiving. It covered only occupational therapy, which basically concentrated on the top portion of his body. Apparently, the top of of Mike's body was the only part the insurance company deemed to be in sufficient need of help. Mike's physical therapists knew the insurance company's decision was wrong-minded, so they graciously continued to help with at least his walking coordination.

Brenda was again assigned a patient advocate to coordinate insurance and the general handling of Mike's case. Stephen participated in the meeting as a second set of eyes and ears and helping to absorb the information threatening to interrupt Mike's recovery. Brenda told the advocate what had already happened concerning the rehab bill several weeks earlier, so the advocate encouraged Brenda to call the insurance company and appeal to them once more. It would be more work, more struggle, more stress.

One morning, after dropping Mike off at outpatient rehab and having had yet another conversation with the patient advocate about her insurance concerns, Brenda drove her car to a nearby Chesapeake Bay lookout to wait for Mike's therapy session to end. She parked the car facing the sparkling water stretching out before her, broke down in tears, and began screaming. "God, I need you to tell me something! Please say something, anything! What am I going to do?" As she sat in the despair of the moment, she reached for one of the books in her pile of "spiritual" resources. It was a small devotional book a friend had given her. Her eyes fell immediately on this passage:

> *Sorrowful One, Death is forever swallowed up in victory! Receive My strength, child. I AM holding you. Despite the pain, I tell you truly: this is a chapter of new beginnings for you and your loved one. I AM mending your heart and you will again know joy… Yes, unspeakable joy.*

You are not wrong to trust Me, so be of good cheer. All will be well. Time and distance are not as your earthly eyes perceive them. Yes, beyond all human hope, and for now in a realm where only I can gain entrance, healing is flowing, I promise.

Yes, you will laugh together—again and again—and it will be in My presence that you do so.

Truly, Father. The words seemed to have tumbled right down from heaven. Brenda returned to pick up Mike feeling encouraged to keep going and believing.

As with all things in her life, Brenda prayed about the insurance situation. She did so despite having little hope of receiving any help from an insurance company that had already said no. But when she called them this time, she spoke to a young woman who was new to the company. Brenda told her the entire story, emphasizing that she had been told by their representatives that they would cover the complete rehab process. The insurance rep said she would need to do a little homework and then call Brenda back, but it would take a few weeks. She said it would be best to hold off on therapies until that time. Brenda returned to prayer.

One of the bills was for Mike's ambulance ride from the hospital to rehab, the one that crashed into a pole. Brenda could not believe they would send a bill for that transport! She called the company and said, "I just received a bill from your company for the ambulance that wrecked on the way to the rehab hospital. I need to speak to a supervisor."

The supervisor came on the phone right away and didn't give Brenda a chance to say even one word. "Mrs. Palmer," he said. "You will never hear from us again." The slate was wiped clean.

Weeks passed before the insurance rep called back. "I have never seen anything quite like this," she said. "But the insurance company is going to pay your entire rehab bill." She explained that when she went back and looked at all the records from their claims, she found recorded phone conversations proving that the insurance company gave out wrong information to the patient advocate. Truly, the advocate was told the policy covered the entire stay and that the Palmers were free to choose any facility in Virginia.

The rep took these recordings to the president of the insurance company, who, after looking at the evidence, agreed the company should and would pay the bill in full—if Brenda would agree to having no written paperwork from the company stating that they were paying the bills.

Brenda agreed, and the bill was completely paid, including the ambulance charges that had already been dropped by the ambulance company.

Though any sense of joy remained far out of Brenda's reach, gratitude was doable, and she often felt washed over with it now. Mike's body was being restored. Money concerns were on the back burner. The wheels were slowly turning on SkyVenture, and Bill seemed to have enough patience and understanding to ride out this storm with them, to find a new way for Mike to continue his work.

The end of the summer was upon them before long, and it was time for Stephen and Amanda to return to their own lives, two bright spots fading into the distance. Brenda would be left with all the responsibilities of getting Mike to and from therapy, walking him through exercises that were part of the process, and enduring his silence and distance. It was time for her and Mike to be alone together in the house again. Their empty nest had never really felt empty after Amanda left for college. Now it would.

Stephen and Amanda with their dad on the day
they returned to their lives, 8/2000

21

Being confident of this very thing, that he which hath begun a good work in you will perform it until the day of Jesus Christ.
— Philippians 1:6 KJV —

Attempting some semblance of a daily routine was a draining process. At what point do you stop making every moment about recovery and just accept the natural unfolding of your circumstances? When do you know that you're as better as you're ever going to be? For Brenda, there was no rest as long as Mike continued to show little indication that he was truly alive inside, behind the dullness of his eyes, the blankness of his stare, and his inability to converse. Her spirit was restless.

There was a heaviness that hung over the entire household, a palpable affliction that shrouded so many things, from paying the bills to simply eating family dinners. They woke up each morning with a new unknown staring them in the face, and they fell into bed each night craving sleep that would relieve them of their present reality. Great sorrow was their relentless, constant companion as they struggled to have even the simplest communication. What was happening to Mike inside his mind? Was he on autopilot, or was his old self trapped in this body, trying to make its way to the surface again?

One afternoon, to do something "normal," Brenda suggested that they drive to visit some close friends who had given birth to a new baby while Mike was in the hospital. She could picture the joy and wonder on Mike's face when he held Stephen for the first time, and later, Amanda. She wondered, with equal parts hope and trepidation, how he would react to the sight of a new baby. But Mike looked upon the tiny, beautiful infant as if it were no more wondrous than a spoon, a sock, a flat stone surrounded by a thousand flat stones. The lack of humanity and connection was obvious and terribly difficult to watch. Someone snapped a picture of Mike and Brenda with the baby. The photo was visual proof of Mike's dispassion.

SEVERAL YEARS BEFORE MIKE'S BRAIN bleed, a group of ladies used to gather monthly at the Palmer home for what began as an evening painting class taught by Brenda. Eventually, they branched out into other crafty activities, but it was primarily a monthly gathering of friends. Everybody brought food, and they gathered in her project room for whatever activity was planned.

Shortly after Mike returned home from rehab, some of the ladies asked Brenda if she was up to resuming their meetings, hoping that spending time with good friends and doing something fun might be a kind of food for her soul. Brenda couldn't imagine "fun," but she went along with the suggestion just because someone asked. Their first attempt was on a Thursday night, but their time was limited by the fact that the music minister at the church, Scott, called Brenda that morning and requested that she bring Mike to choir rehearsal for a few minutes that evening. The choir wanted to "sing and play over Mike." Brenda didn't have a clue what that meant, but she agreed, because she knew Scott cared about them and had their best interest at heart.

Another good friend, Eric, offered to drive them to the church for this affair. It was a small gesture, but it felt good to Brenda to be the chauffeured and to be in the company of friends for any sort of outing. As they drove along, Eric asked how things were going. Without thinking, Brenda answered, "You know, we're pretty sure we have figured out why people kill themselves." She knew it was a shocking thing to say, but unbridled honesty was the new norm. Their friend appeared unfazed as he continued driving down the road.

From the church parking lot, they walked together into the large sanctuary and sat in the front row looking at the semicircle stage where the massive choir was gathered and practicing for Sunday service. There were also two visiting, well-known musicians accompanying the band, one playing clarinet and the other a trumpet. Their instruments reflected the overhead lights, and as they shifted with the music, little gleams traveled up the smooth spaces between the keys like shooting stars.

Brenda had always felt like the sanctuary, with its massive domed ceiling and arena seating, was more like a convention center than a church. Most of the regulars formed small communities based on their little carved-out spots in the colossal room. She suffered it only because she and Mike had made real friends here. Even though the music was something to behold, Brenda felt her best worshiping had never been done in church anyway. It was done in small and intimate gatherings outside church on Sunday mornings. For her, "church" was conversing with a group of trusted friends over coffee. It was beach breakfasts and walking with Sandy by the water. It was community formed by spending time together and showing up for one another when the time came. Church was everywhere and a way of life. Music only played a supporting role in helping her feel close to God.

After a few minutes, Scott asked Mike and Brenda to come to the platform as he reminded the musicians and choir about what had happened to Mike. Most of them knew the story, having heard it a number of times from the pulpit. The minister then explained to them that he believed music, both vocal and instrumental, could have a healing effect. He wanted the musicians and singers to surround Mike on the stage as they made their joyful noises. He began by asking everyone to bow their heads as he prayed a simple prayer requesting that God bring healing to Mike through their music. Then they began to play.

For several minutes—Brenda couldn't say how long—she and Mike were encircled by music. The music was no different from the usual music they would hear at Sunday services. Nothing extraordinary happened, no tent-healing miracles that stripped away all the pain in the blink of an eye. Was that the intention? Brenda couldn't say, but being at the center of the music, being the purpose of it, made her feel that she and Mike were loved and cared for by so many people. After the singing stopped, Scott prayed another prayer before Brenda and Mike thanked the group and were dropped off at their house to go to bed. She didn't say a word about the experience to Mike, and he certainly didn't have any commentary either.

The next morning, when they woke up, Mike looked changed to Brenda. His dull, flat expression was replaced with light and life. It was as if a switch had been flipped behind Mike's eyes. The change was so stark that Brenda realized the denial she'd been experiencing up until that point—the refusal to accept just how lifeless Mike had looked since coming out of his coma.

Later that day, as Mike was resting on the bed, he began to talk without prompting. "When I was in rehab," he said, "someone stole a box of brain fragments from me."

Brenda had no idea what he was talking about, but when she tried to get him to explain, he couldn't. He said he didn't know what else to say. He tried a different way: "I know I had a box of brain fragments. Someone stole them." Pressed again to explain, he said it didn't make any sense to him either, but he kept insisting it was absolutely true. The comment was uncharacteristically cryptic and poetic for Mike. It was also conversational. For a moment, he was talking to her.

With a sense of wonder and hope, Brenda left the room to let Mike nap. While he was sleeping, a woman from church called. Helen and her husband, Bob, had worked together with Mike and Brenda on a marriage committee at church. Bob was one of the microphone-wielding men who had led in prayer that first Sunday morning after Mike's brain hemorrhage. They were some of the first to show up at the hospital, and they came to visit faithfully, day after day. Helen was known for her dedicated prayer commitments to people. As they were talking now, she told Brenda, "I have been taking communion all week for someone, not sure who. I believe I was to pray and fast for someone's 'fragmentation.' I'm not sure what that means, but I am sure that was the specific word—fragmentation."

Brenda didn't know what to make of any of it, what it all meant. She believed, however, that during the past twenty-four hours, she had witnessed something supernatural. Whatever it was, it brought a bit of life back into Mike's face and, by extension, his very soul.

22

*Consider it all joy, my brethren, when you encounter various trials,
knowing that the testing of your faith produces endurance. And let
endurance have its perfect result, that you may be perfect and complete,
lacking in nothing.*

— James 1:2–4 NASB —

As far back as she could remember, Brenda was always drawn to creative pursuits—music, arts, and crafts, and even conversation and teaching—all of which she raised to an art form in the many church communities she had called home. One room in the house was filled to bursting with evidence of this former version of herself: hundreds of little bottles of paints in every hue, paraphernalia to make beautiful stamp designs, curly-edged craft scissors, flower-arranging goodies, candles, oil lamps, decorating books, ribbons, stencils, brushes—all of it now collecting dust. So were the countless folders overflowing with handouts from classes she had taught over the years at church, classes for young women, classes on how to live better lives and how to love husbands and be good "keepers of the home."

Though they were stuffed full and thick like Dagwood sandwiches, all of these folders somehow seemed empty to Brenda now. She couldn't remember why she had ever believed she had anything to teach anyone. She didn't know how to make her own daily existence better. Who was she to tell others how to do it? And the things she advised them to do! Why did it matter how you set the table or whether you lit a candle? How could she have taught such things with certainty and passion just a few weeks earlier, when now she was struggling with just getting through the day, and sleep was the only place where she could find relief?

With the kids gone, every day was not only a slog but also filled with problems that left Brenda feeling like she needed more than one miracle. She needed heaps of them. She felt isolated and alone, with Mike unable to advise her in any way. Putting up her hands, calling a halt to the latest impossibility, and saying, "Let's pray" became a daily affair. She often grabbed Mike's hands and prayed some version or another of this prayer: "Lord, we're in trouble, and we need you to help us. We don't know what to do. Please tell us what to do. If you don't help us, we're not going to make it. We don't know how to do this. Please give us what we need." Brenda did this "911 prayer" persistently and repetitively, until it became a way of life for them. She had no other help, and if God was anywhere, she needed him to be with her. He was her only hope.

One evening, after Mike had been struggling at his computer to no avail, he and Brenda sat in the den, again going through the excruciating exercise of trying to get past the hours leading up to bedtime. Brenda was tired of empty, lonely, agonizing feelings. Worse, she was terrified that this was now their life. Everything that once defined them as a couple was different, and now what were they going to do? Overcome with this fear, she grabbed Mike's hands and pleaded with God to help them. The words poured out of the most private parts of her soul. Mike let her pray in this way and held her hands, but he did not show any other sign of participating.

Afterward, as they sat looking at each other, the idea suddenly came to her that they should put on their old clothes and go clean up Mike's shop. It was a detached garage in their backyard that was his domain. Brenda had helped Mike clean up the shop here and there in the past, but it was never something she suggested or volunteered to do. The few times she ventured there after Mike's AVM rupture, she felt like she couldn't breathe from the sight of all the rusting tools and half-finished projects lying unused and forgotten.

Volunteering to head into that place seemed like a kind of torture session, looking at so many reminders of the Mike that once was. Maybe this was a way to reconnect him to himself, like breadcrumbs tossed out to his starving soul. Would he find some of his "stolen fragments" here perhaps? Whether or not that was the case, she had no compulsion to dissect this response to her prayer, because she knew the idea to visit the workshop wasn't her own. Going

Mike's workshop

into the workshop at least gave them something different to do until bedtime. And if it could somehow help Mike in his recovery, Brenda was willing to do it. She didn't really care what it was they did: Anything was fine with her as long as they made progress. It wasn't an act of mindless "moving on" to simply fight inertia. It was an act of constantly searching for little footholds that would help Mike climb out of the deep hole.

Brenda thought of a Bible verse that summed it all up: "Dear friends, do you think you'll get anywhere in this if you learn all the right words but never do anything? Does merely talking about faith indicate that a person has it? Isn't it obvious that God-talk without God-acts is outrageous nonsense?"

Mike had never previously relished the idea of cleaning that shop, and there was no reason to think his poor opinion of the chore was changed by a brain injury. Still, he numbly and obediently did most anything Brenda asked of him now, so the two of them headed up to the bedroom to change into work clothes. Then they dragged themselves out the door, across the lawn under the towering trees, and into the shop. Once inside, Mike stood blankly waiting for Brenda to tell him what to do. This was his domain, but now he appeared clueless, and the sight of him standing amid his tools, projects, and gadgetry, waiting to be ordered into action, was difficult for Brenda to see. She pushed past the feelings and started on one corner of the room, pulling items off shelves and making piles of things to throw away. "Can I throw this away?" she asked. "How about this?" Over and over, Mike said, "Yes." Once the kind of frugal guy who kept almost everything just in case it should be needed later, he let her toss anything she wanted to toss. Did he have no feeling for any of it?

For maybe a half hour, Brenda told her once-brilliant rocket-scientist husband what to do and watched as he obediently put each item in the appropriate place. There was no way they were going to make a serious dent, but at least it was a start. When she couldn't bear the emotional pain of the experience any longer, she suggested they turn in for the night. She shut off the light and held Mike's hand as they walked across the backyard under the weight of the stars and the bent shadows of the trees, moving in silence toward their only place of peace: sleep.

In the first hours following Mike's brain bleed, Brenda had no idea the endurance that would be required of them, how many more laps were to come. There was nobody standing outside his hospital room with a sign that said, "Lap 1. You have 500 more to go." Now she sometimes thought back to that strange call from Lib in the days before the AVM rupture. "… Make it plain upon tablets," went the Bible verse Lib called to share, "that he may run that readeth it." Now Brenda constantly watched for signs of how many laps were still ahead of them.

Over the course of the next few months, she and Mike continued to trudge out to the shop when the nights were long and slow, gradually restoring it to order. One of the nights they were cleaning, Brenda asked Mike to put a big nail into one of the upper studs of the garage so that she could hang up an oil-changing container. He dutifully climbed atop a stepstool and tried to worry the nail into place. However, among the strange artifacts left behind by Mike's AVM rupture was his inability to release not only *objects* but also *energy* from his right hand. He couldn't throw a ball, and he couldn't cause a hammer to make contact with a nail. Each time he swung the hammer, it stopped about a half-inch shy of the nail. Now he tried a different tack, starting with the tiniest little hummingbird swings at the nail, which he was able to build up into a partial swing within a few seconds, one that made contact with the nail.

As Brenda stood beneath him, taking in the sight of him in his old work jeans and T-shirt, so painfully normal-looking and yet so far from it, these words came into her head: *I want to see him doing these things more than you do. I love him more than you do.*

She was startled. Those were not her thoughts, and they angered her.

She had to restrain herself from screaming, "No, you don't!"

Yet in the days ahead, she found herself clinging to those words. She forced herself to reflect on them when she felt alone. In them, she saw God's stated plan for a good outcome. It gave her some hope for the future and allowed her to rest a little, knowing her husband was in the hands of a heavenly Father who loved him more than she did. Whenever doubt crept up on her, she would just picture Mike standing on that ladder with his hammer, figuring out a new way.

The days turned into weeks, and the weeks turned into months, Mike recovering small slivers of his former self a little at a time. The shop was all cleaned up and organized now. That glimmer of something-ness in Mike's remained only a glimmer but could be seen more often. He was more responsive in conversation, if not animated. They began going out for meals again with friends. These social situations became less stilted and awkward each time but not dramatically so. The waning of discomfort was equal parts acceptance and recovery—acceptance of a new normal, and recovery that was visible only if one stood back from the situation a bit for a wider view of it all.

By the time the New Year arrived, it was clear that Mike was more awake to his surroundings and situation. Brenda decided to tell Mike the story of Spencer once again. She had told him before, but he had no actual memory of him and his family.

"Mike," she began, "there was a young man in the room with you at the hospital. His father prayed over you. Did you know that?"

Mike shook his head no and waited for the rest. Brenda told him every part: Spencer's mother receiving a friend's request to pray for Mike, how she asked for his name so she could pray specifically. She talked of seeing Spencer unconscious in his bed, of the pain and loss his parents experienced while still showing beautiful compassion and encouragement toward Mike. When she described Spencer's dad praying for Mike, when she talked of Spencer's young son, and when she finally told him Spencer passed, Mike's eyes filled with tears.

Many people with brain injuries are more prone to crying, and this was certainly the case for Mike, but unlike some brain-injury survivors, his tears were seldom disconnected from reality. They always had an impetus. Still, the crying was a new thing for those who knew him. Mike was never one to cry before the injury. Brenda looked deeper into Mike's tears now and wanted to know about them. She listened to him as he tried to explain: "It's...k-k-kuh-kind of...*deep sigh*...it's strange for me...th, th, that...it's strange for me that *deep sigh, furrowed brow*...there's a whole s-s-set... a whole set....*sigh* a set of—a whole lot of people I haven't met that are...*reaching for words, pursed lips, frustrated sigh.* that are tied to us forever." Every time Brenda recounted Spencer's story after that day, she saw Mike's eyes fill with tears. She knew that he felt a profound interest when he heard the story. She knew he wondered why his life was spared while this young man's was not. Brenda didn't have the answers. Neither did Mike. Nobody did. It was a crushing mystery that demanded a lot of faith in God, but not nearly as much as it demanded of Spencer's parents, Kathie and Dave. Brenda wondered about them often: How were they doing? What did their faith look like now? Would they ever want to meet Mike? Could they see him without reliving those terrible days? Would it hurt too much?

Brenda so wanted Mike to meet them. It wasn't only because of Mike's comments. Partly, it was because she truly did feel connected to Kathie. In the early days of Mike's recovery, Kathie saw it all. She saw as much as anyone, and more than most. She and Dave had prayed for Mike. They had walked near Brenda through the darkest spaces of life. Their daughters had communed in grief while walking the corridors beyond midnight. The small and delicate conversations between two grown women who knew each other not one whit but saw deep into each other's souls, bound them together forever.

One day, after many weeks of thinking about the idea, Brenda picked up the phone and called the friend who had asked Kathie to pray for Mike.

"Do you think it would be possible for Mike to meet Kathie and Dave?" she asked. "I'd like to see them, too."

The mutual friend reached out to Kathie, who graciously answered that she would absolutely love to meet Mike. She invited them to her home. A week later, when that day arrived, the Palmers steered their car around the soft curves of the roads leading away from Poquoson and into Williamsburg. A short gravel driveway led from the road and up to the gray, square, clapboard house with blue shutters and a blue door.

Kathie stood at the top of the porch steps, beaming. As Mike and Brenda walked toward her, she burst into tears.

"Look what God has done!" she exclaimed.

Her reaction was so typical of the woman Brenda remembered. She was genuinely overjoyed to see Mike, standing upright and coming toward her. She was excited to see a much more healed man than she ever imagined he could be.

"I just assumed you would be in a wheelchair," she explained.

For the next couple of hours, Brenda and Kathie sat and talked like old friends.

Over the coming months, Mike and Brenda spent a few more evenings with Dave and Kathie. Each visit was an uplifting and encouraging experience, and every time, they all prayed together for Mike's complete recovery. They did so with unspoken understanding and deeply felt passion. Brenda and Mike marveled at their profound grace and faith.

MANY OF THE WOMEN IN the church had heard of Brenda because of the classes she taught, but only close friends knew Mike, the thoughtful engineer. Seemingly overnight, Mike was thrust into the spotlight and became the miracle story. It seemed that everyone knew who he was and felt as though they were a part of his story. Mike and Brenda were often stopped on their way into or out of church by complete strangers wanting to know how Mike was doing. Ron was responsible for that: Mike and his recovery had become a frequent staple of Ron's sermons, as were the stories of a few other individuals dealing with severe illnesses or tragedies.

A woman in the congregation named Carol was the next in line after Mike for this dubious honor. Carol and her husband sat close to Mike's and Brenda's usual section in the large sanctuary. After Mike and Brenda began regularly attending church again, Carol came to them one Sunday morning, introduced herself, and said she had been praying for them. She explained that she had a heartfelt understanding of what had happened to Mike, because Carol's own mother had also had an AVM. A short time later, Carol was diagnosed with cancer. Mike and Brenda, feeling great camaraderie with her, began praying for her and would often speak with Carol and her husband between services.

One Wednesday evening, one of the pastors announced that Carol was not doing well and that she wasn't expected to live past the end of the week. Brenda was shocked. She was unaware of Carol's seemingly fast decline. That night, she had a two-part dream about Carol. In the dream, Brenda was standing in a hallway at Bethel Temple when she was approached by an elderly woman she had known for many years but had not seen in a long time. Her name was Sarah. Years earlier, when they served together on a board for a mission organization, Brenda had come to think of Sarah as the godliest person she had ever met. In the dream, Brenda somehow knew that Sarah was aware of both Mike's situation and Carol's illness. Sarah looked beautiful and appeared younger than Brenda remembered. She looked Brenda square in the eye and said, "This is not Russian roulette, you know." Then the scene suddenly shifted, and Brenda was in a room down the hall where she saw Carol lying on a large bed. Brenda climbed up on the bed next to her and said, "Carol, what is this like for you?"

When Brenda woke, she knew three things: She knew that Carol was going to die soon.

She knew that Sarah was instructing her not to equate Carol's outcome with Mike's but instead to continue praying and asking for Mike to be healed. And she knew that from now on, she was to let people talk about their illnesses, tragedies, and their impending death without fear that doing so would indicate a lack of faith.

23

For you have need of endurance, so that when you have done the will of God, you may receive what was promised.
— Hebrews 10:36 ESV —

One of the loudest reminders of Mike and Brenda's once promising, now precarious future, was SkyVenture. In March of 2001, ten months after Mike's AVM rupture, Bill Kitchen called with news that he had received a bite: a customer willing to purchase the first SkyVenture wind tunnel. This was more than two years after contractors completed the hugely successful prototype in Orlando.

The news was both exciting and terrifying, as Mike was not yet drawing with AutoCAD, the computer-aided drafting software that was a mainstay in his work. Mechanically, he just couldn't get his body and mind to coordinate for the task yet. Typing was still a hunt-and-peck process, and gripping, clicking, and maneuvering a mouse were beyond his present skills.

Bill asked both Brenda and Mike to fly to Florida to discuss their involvement in the project. All of the fabrication work on the previous tunnel had been done in Virginia, so all seemed to be in agreement that it would be quickest and easiest to fabricate the next one there, too, using the same resources. Mike didn't seem at all nervous, but Brenda was. During the flight to Florida, she realized that even though she wasn't sure how they were going to do another tunnel now, figuring it out would surely be easier than recovering from a brain injury.

Mike and Brenda sat down with Bill and some of his new employees to make plans. This was Brenda's first exposure to this type of business discussion. She took detailed notes, knowing Mike would need them and couldn't take them for himself. Her stomach tightened as Bill looked at them both and asked, "Can you build another tunnel? Can you do this?"

Mike's tempo in replying was slow and broken, in a way that everyone pretended not to find uncomfortable. But he was also determined. "Yes," he said, somewhat loudly. "Uh, uh, uh"—*closing his eyes, frustrated sigh*—"I...I'd like to...g-g-give...like to give...give it"—*opening his eyes, piercing gaze*—"I can do that." He and Brenda left Florida with a $250,000 check to begin the preliminary work. Brenda wasn't sure Mike could do it, neither at the pace nor in the manner the client might expect, but he simply had to do it. Mike had taken a tremendous financial risk when he left his job to do the SkyVenture project, and now failing just wasn't an option. Despite already feeling as though they were in over their head, Brenda leaned hard on her faith, trusting that whatever was supposed to happen, would happen.

The wind tunnel was to be built in Malaysia, with SkyVenture supplying the guts, and the customer being responsible for the rest. The shipping deadline was set for the early part of September 2001. That gave Mike six months to do his thing. As soon as they arrived home, Mike and Brenda deposited the check and began the process of visiting each one of the contractors that had worked on the first tunnel, to see who would be willing to work again with Mike despite his deficits.

Their first visit was to Bay Welding, the company that had done the most extensive work of the steel fabrication. Mike Eppard, the owner assured them that he was more than willing to do it all again. He had visited Mike in the hospital on a number of occasions and was anxious to help out. They next contacted the owner of Metal Concepts, the sheet-metal company that had made the odd-shaped ductwork needed for the tunnel. After reviewing the blueprints, that company's owner also agreed to do another tunnel. Finally, they contacted George Sydnor from NASA, the electrical engineer. He took a little more time coming onboard, asking Mike quite a series of questions before committing to the project. Brenda figured he must need assurance that Mike was capable of doing the work that would be required to make the project successful. She and Mike both understood. In the end, all those who were asked, heartily agreed to partner with Mike on the second tunnel.

Over the next several months, Mike and Brenda visited fabrication sites, answered questions, corrected drawings, and prayed. Then they prayed some more. Each day was filled with challenges, as Mike attempted to get back into a serious work schedule. Brenda stayed in the office with him and helped in any way she could.

Mike's right hand still showed lingering paralysis, so Brenda typed most of his emails for him, having him give the okay before she hit send. He usually insisted that she delete anything of an emotional nature: Her tone tended to be more personal and could come across as sensitive when she had the sense someone was questioning Mike's decisions or opinions. That protectiveness came through in her emails. Mike, on the other hand, saw it as business and was vigilant in weeding out anything she wrote that he deemed to be unprofessional.

It hardly seemed possible that their situation could become more stressful than it already was, but the SkyVenture demands introduced a new layer of agony. Brenda was in over her head, trying to navigate the engineering world, feigning that she belonged there so as not to scare off—or lose—the client. She felt she had no choice but to be smack in the middle of the madness.

It was both a blessing and a curse that Mike was hundreds of miles away from Bill Kitchen and the prying eyes of anyone else in the company. The distance meant they could not see the enormous nature of what they were dealing with every waking hour, the dozens of plates they seemed to be spinning at once. Ironically, the long distance made empathy impossible, too. It seemed to Brenda that at any moment, all the plates could come crashing down. Trying to accomplish almost any task was like trying to cut through gristle with a butter knife. The tension was high, and Brenda often felt panicked. She knew in her bones that they were never going to manage it all without supernatural help. When Mike was unable to complete a task, find a file, or remember how to perform some computer function, she got in the habit of grabbing his hands and saying, "Let's pray."

"Lord, Mike can't find this drawing. If you don't help us, we're in trouble."

"Lord, Mike can't remember how to do this function."

"Lord, I don't know how we're going to make a living if you don't give Mike what he needs. Please help us."

The act of praying felt different now. Brenda, the little girl who'd once marched herself down to the front of Oral Baptist Church to get saved, was now lacking that childlike certainty. She realized, for the first time in her life, that faith and certainty were not one and the same.

Gone was the sense of utmost confidence that her prayers would be answered. Eating at the edges of those prayers was doubt. Panic, fear, and distress woven through every word of her prayers and lingered after each "Amen."

She found that staying in the room to "help" Mike after these prayers usually just muddied things. To relieve the stress, she learned to simply walk away after they prayed. Before returning, she would give Mike plenty of time to solve the dilemma at hand. Without fail, every time she returned, the latest crisis was resolved, and Mike was already on to the next task. The act of going through this process over and over again forced her to see that her Father could be trusted. Her fingers were slowly being uncurled from around every problem, and she was learning to quit trying so hard to fix everything.

They were entering a new level of partnership in the rawest and truest sense of the word.

Brenda learned to read Mike's face during conference calls, not an easy task in light of how much animation Mike still lacked. In those calls and in meetings, she often spoke for him and tried to express things she felt he wanted to get across, using the words she thought he would use. For the most part, everyone on the receiving end went along with this awkward arrangement. What choice did they have? SkyVenture needed Mike's input, and this was the only way they were going to get it.

During the years leading up to Mike's AVM rupture, Brenda had often watched him deal with deadlines, cost overruns, fabrication issues, contractor personalities, and errors and corrections in drawings. "On time and under budget" was the common charge in his world. So was high pressure. Now, as they worked on building a structure that had been built only once before, there was the added pressure of a brain injury and its residual effects. Brenda sometimes looked at herself in the mirror and asked aloud, "How are you surviving? How is this not killing you?" Then she would shake her head and keep going, knowing deep down what the answer was. It was her hourly dependence on God.

One morning, she was cooking breakfast on the stove and going through the mental exercise of again trying to face the days. "God, how could you allow one of your children to suffer like this?" she asked. "I would never let one of my kids go through this if I could help it." She really didn't know whether she or Mike was the child in this scenario. Then these words leaped into her head: "I know the end, and you don't."

The words certainly weren't hers, but she knew what they meant. When Mike came to sit down to breakfast, she told him what had just happened. "It would be like if Amanda called us suddenly and said she wanted to quit school. You know how ridiculous that is, because she would never do such a thing! What would you tell her?"

"You can't quit!'" Mike answered.

"Exactly. You would tell her that, because you know more than she does about the importance of staying in school, right?"

He nodded.

"That's what those words meant, Mike. God knows more about why you're suffering than we do, and He has reasons for this process that we are incapable of understanding, just like Amanda is incapable of fully understanding why she should stay in school, because she hasn't experienced enough of life yet to allow her to fully understand the value of not quitting."

Of course, neither of them could imagine Amanda dropping out of school—she was far too responsible, mature, and intelligent to even consider it—but two weeks later, they got a call from her asking to do just that. Amanda explained that she was having a difficult time being around college students who simply did not understand the real-life stuff she now knew because of her dad's illness. She felt like she needed to move on and do something more important with her life. They cried with her. They told her they completely understood how she felt, the isolation of the experience being all too familiar to them. Then Mike told Amanda that she could not quit, that he would not allow it, and that if she didn't understand why, she would just have to trust him and her mom and do what they were advising. Someday, she'd understand.

Amanda had no reason to distrust her parents' wisdom. They had never led her astray. And perhaps partly out of respect for her dad's wishes—what a blessing that he had opinions, could voice them, and would cry with her in her moment of struggle—she stayed the course. The topic of leaving school never came up again.

Eventually, things around the house started breaking and needing repair as things in an older house are bound to do. Engineers don't like to spend money on repairmen, a trait that Brenda once found irritating. Now she used it to her advantage. With each needed repair—hot-water heater, dryer, dishwasher, water pump, radiator, busted pipe, and on, and on and on—she went to Mike, who would attempt the repairs. He reacted just like "old Mike," assuming that he could do it. Each time, Brenda thought that she might be asking a little more than his abilities would allow, she reminded herself that her only role was to ask God for help.

Again, when she got to feeling overwhelmed, she would grab Mike's hands and say, "Let's pray." Other times she did her praying alone and under her breath, for example while Mike crawled under the house or went to the hardware store. She watched his partially crippled hand clumsily work through each repair. Once, when an upstairs doorknob needed replacing, he attempted the repair with what she knew to be the wrong tool. Brenda had seen him do this type of repair many times in the past, so she knew what he would normally use. When she suggested the correct replacement, he looked at her with instant acknowledgment. He had simply forgotten about that particular tool and needed a reminder. He always managed and slowly, maddeningly, he regained a great deal of his former abilities. However, new challenges were always just around the corner, some bigger than others.

In the early days after rehab, one of those bigger challenges was driving. Dr. Ross, at the rehab center, had not felt that driving was a good idea for Mike just yet. Instead, he put a date on the calendar a couple of months down the road when he thought it would be safe for him to try. Driving was extremely important to Mike, and he frequently asked Brenda if he could do it. The question tore at her heart. She did not like playing keeper of the keys and having to say no to him as though he were a child. Finally, a couple of weeks before Dr. Ross's target date for giving driving a whirl, Brenda cracked.

She and Mike were walking out of the grocery store less than a half-mile from their house when she asked him if he'd like to drive them home. He perked up noticeably, came around to the driver's side, and confidently took the wheel.

When they arrived at the house, Brenda asked, "How did it feel to drive for the first time?"

Mike grinned triumphantly. "It's not the first time," he said.

She looked at him, unable to believe her ears. "Who let you drive?"

"Amanda."

In typical fashion, Brenda wasn't upset by the secret—amused was more like it—but she sure wanted to know the story. Amanda later told her that she had been driving her dad around the back roads of Poquoson one day, decided to stop the car, and told him he could drive. They decided it would be their secret until Brenda turned over the keys.

One morning in the early spring of 2001, Brenda was sitting with a group of friends at a Bible study down the road from her house when she received a call from Mike on her cell phone. He was obviously in distress and unable to say much of anything except "seizure." Robin was with her at the meeting, so the two of them ran out to the car and started driving in the direction of where they thought Mike might be. Brenda knew he was working out at the gym with Kevin that morning and planned to get a haircut afterward. She didn't know whether he was at the gym, the hairdresser's, or somewhere in between. Instead of hanging up and calling the hairdresser, she kept Mike on the phone, knowing that it would help for him to hear her voice, reassuring him that he was not alone. She asked yes-or-no questions and figured that he most likely was sitting in the parking lot at the salon.

When they arrived, they found Mike sitting in his car, quite shaken up. His seizure had subsided, and he seemed to be able to walk. Brenda walked him to the passenger's side of the car and drove directly to the emergency room, where he spent the next several hours being checked from head to toe.

After he was released to go home, Mike told Brenda that the seizure hit him just after he drove into the parking lot and turned off the car. He described to her how his hands were on the steering wheel when his body started shaking, giving him the sensation that some sort of motor was controlling him. The next thing he knew, he was paralyzed on the right side of his body, just as he'd been right after the AVM rupture. Once the seizure subsided, he was somehow able to dial his phone.

Not long before the seizure, Mike had been seen for a regular checkup with his neurosurgeon, who told him that he was fascinated with his case and wanted to see him one more time, just to see Mike's progress. He also wanted to transition Mike smoothly to the neurologist. The appointment was moved up due to the seizure.

The new doctor concluded during his exam that Mike needed a higher dose of the anti-seizure medicine he had been taking since his AVM rupture. He said the seizure was caused by irritation from the surgery scar and that Mike needed a different medicine. Though no lasting damage was done, it was a harrowing experience. Mike was again restricted from driving for a few weeks while the medicine saturated his bloodstream. This setback greatly distressed him, but it couldn't be helped.

Meanwhile, the stressors of working daily on SkyVenture continued. By summer, it was time for the wind tunnel to be built in Malaysia. A construction manager, Todd, was hired and remained in close contact with Mike, reaching out to him many times a day with questions and clarifications. At some point, Todd wanted to bring in a fiberglass expert to check on a design choice Mike made for the inlet at the bottom of the tunnel. The inlet, similar in shape to the back ends of the space shuttle, consisted of ten large panels bolted together. Each panel was quite heavy and over ten feet in length. On the Florida wind tunnel, the hot sun had caused bubbling on this inlet, so for the Malaysia tunnel, Mike came up with a fix that involved layering fiberglass. He was so confident in the fix that he saw no need for a fiberglass expert. Todd reluctantly deferred to Mike's decision, and construction moved forward.

For construction of the fiberglass component, Mike looked to a former colleague from his MicroCraft days, John Lowe. He and Mike had worked together on a number of projects in the past, and Mike had confidence in John's ability. Though John was new to the method of fiberglass-layering that Mike wanted, he assured him that he would have no problem getting up to speed on it.

Of course, there is no such thing as construction without glitches. The new machine that was needed to make the inlet pieces arrived late, pushing back the construction to Labor Day weekend. To solve the problem and get the schedule back on track, John tried subcontracting with a local fiberglass boat-builder to finish making the pieces for the tunnel, but the employees simply refused to work over their holiday.

Todd was scheduled to arrive shortly after the holiday to start packing up components of the tunnel into the shipping crates headed for Malaysia, but it was now looking as though the parts might not be ready by the time he arrived. Mike wasn't happy about the delay, so he and Brenda visited the boat-building company to check on progress. John and the company owner assured him that, although the schedule was extremely tight, they would make it work.

Sure enough, the pieces were delivered to the shipping site in Williamsburg the day before Todd was to arrive. Mike and Brenda traveled to the site themselves to make sure things were a go. To their dismay, they found that even though the fiberglass pieces had been delivered, they had been improperly stacked, causing a piece on the bottom of the stack to break. Both felt sick, knowing there was not enough time to get it repaired before Todd's arrival. It would need to be taken back to the boat shop for repair.

Brenda suspected that this would give Todd an excuse to question Mike's decision concerning the details of the fiberglass, which would almost certainly seem like a taped-together solution. She felt that Mike's reputation was on the line, so she immediately called John Lowe to let him know what had happened. He apologized profusely and offered to come out the next day to fix the piece, but tomorrow was too late. Tomorrow, Todd would arrive. Tomorrow, Mike would look incompetent. Mike seemed unconcerned, but Brenda was beside herself.

After their 40-minute drive home, Brenda went to their bedroom feeling spent and simply dropped to her knees. She was so disappointed in God. She had done everything she knew to do, and still it was not good enough. She felt responsible for Mike's reputation and didn't see any way for the situation to have a good outcome. Through her tears, she said, "God, you know the situation. You got us into this mess, and it's your problem. Please do something about it. There's nothing else I can do. I've done all I can."

Brenda knew how many times God answered her prayers, but this one seemed impossible, even for God. In that moment, she forgot the oceans, seashores, and mountains—profound wonders made possible through this supernatural force that she now beseeched for help. His mighty power didn't feel mighty at all. She was so consumed with her own desperation that she had no idea what was going through Mike's mind as they fell into bed that night.

The next morning, Mike went to his scheduled gym workout. Brenda slipped into the bathtub to try to soak away some of her stress when the phone rang. It was Stephen on the line, asking if she was watching the news. Did she know what was happening in New York? She had no idea. "Two planes have crashed into the World Trade Center," he said.

"Two planes is not an accident," Brenda answered. As she hung up, Mike came through the front door, and they immediately turned on the television. Together, they watched in horror as the first tower came crashing down. Brenda felt like all of creation was going up in smoke. Then she saw that the second tower was on fire.

"Mike, is that second tower going to fall?" she asked.

"Yes," he said.

They stayed glued to the television, frozen with shock. More sorrow and defeat pressed upon the great sadness Brenda was already buried beneath. She felt gutted. Shipping containers and tunnel pieces and fiberglass didn't matter anymore. The whole country seemed to be coming apart.

Later that afternoon, Todd called to say he was not coming after all. His plane in Dallas had just taxied out onto the runway when all flights in the United States were canceled. His mind wasn't on the wind tunnel either. The country had bigger fish to fry, and it would be a week before Todd arrived to oversee the packing of the shipping containers.

After the wind-tunnel components were shipped to Malaysia and the construction process began, Mike often received middle-of-the-night calls

SkyVenture inlet assembly

from Todd. He rang with questions and wanting clarification on various aspects of the tunnel assembly. One such call involved the tunnel's wire floor, which consisted of a crisscrossing of cables that formed the mesh floor of the tunnel. The design would be different from the Orlando tunnel, which needed frequent wire replacement after it was in operation. This was because the wires of the floor passed through holes in the sides of the walls, and the friction kept causing the wires to fray.

Before his illness, Mike had come up with a new design plan for the floor, using a series of pulleys to relieve stress on the wires. However, he had never written instructions for stringing this new floor. Now Todd was calling to request the guidelines. Mike stared at the computer screen, knowing this was going to require speech he did not have. Brenda, recognizing the look of frustration on his face, told Todd they would send the instructions as soon as possible.

When they hung up the phone, she stared at the screen. "What are we going to do?" she asked. Knowing that she was quite good at teaching anything she could understand, Brenda said, "Mike, walk me through this, and let's see if I can write the instructions. You must help me understand how to do this."

With a lot of questions, clarification, screen pointing, and broken conversation, they slowly, point by point, step by step, made their way through the process of stringing the floor with the new pulley system. A few hours later, they successfully sent Todd a set of instructions. No one at SkyVenture ever knew what that document had cost them in energy and anxiety.

24

To love another person is to see the face of God.
— Victor Hugo —

In the months to follow, Mike and Brenda left the house more often and started to move beyond the pain. They even discovered there was something helpful they could do with it. There were other hurting people out there! As Mike and Brenda sat in church one Sunday morning, a couple who sat nearby asked them if they would visit the couple's friend in the hospital ICU.

The friend, a young woman, had undergone surgery to remove a brain tumor. Something had gone wrong, and now she was in serious condition. She and her family needed encouragement. Mike and Brenda had never met the couple making this request. Nor did they know the woman in the hospital. Later that week, as they walked up to the information desk in the intensive care unit at the Norfolk hospital with the woman's name written on a piece of paper, they knew it was an unorthodox move. Why would they be allowed access to someone in the ICU who they didn't even know? They were discovering newfound boldness and the ability to step into the pain of others that they had not known before. Surprisingly, no questions were asked, and they were ushered into the room where the woman was lying in the hospital bed with a tracheotomy tube, her hands drawn up. She stared at them without recognition, as did the other three family members in the room.

The patient, Carolyn, lived within a few miles of their house. During the couple of years after she was released from the hospital, Mike and Brenda made frequent visits to her home, doing anything they could imagine might bring optimism and light to her overwhelming existence. Her face would light up each time she saw Mike. She loved seeing him. He represented hope, the prospect of getting better, and he understood.

One day when they arrived to visit Carolyn, they were met at the door by her mother, who had moved in to help with caregiving. She was distressed because Carolyn had been expressing a desire to end her life. Mike walked over to the bed and haltingly spoke to her.

"I understand how you feel. I have felt that way. I could not do that because I have kids and that would hurt them, but I understand."

Carolyn's eyes filled with tears as she thanked Mike for validating her and not demanding that she stop saying what she was feeling. As Brenda witnessed this exchange, she saw that people who are hurting should be allowed and even encouraged to speak the truth they are experiencing, without fear of judgment. That alone could bring its own relief.

On another occasion, someone on the church staff called to report that one of the pastors, Terry, had been in a serious automobile accident. Mike and Brenda had been out to dinner with Terry and his wife, Kathy, the night prior. During dinner, Terry had remarked how odd he found it that Brenda and Mike dated events in their lives from the moment of Mike's injury, referring to everything as *before the injury* or *after the injury.*

As Terry pulled out of his subdivision early that next morning, a large dump truck had plowed into his car, triggering the airbag deployment, crushing his hands, and causing extensive head trauma. Because of their experience with brain trauma, Mike and Brenda were asked to come to the hospital to support Kathy.

Brenda grabbed several personal items, placing them in a Ziploc pouch to hand to Kathy when they arrived: toothbrush, toothpaste, comb, mouthwash, hand lotion, wet towelettes—items she knew Kathy would need but would not have brought. As they entered the same step-down room Mike had occupied just a few months earlier, the smell of plastics, cleaning solution, and fear hit Brenda in the face, startling her and stopping her in her tracks. Mike was oblivious to the fact that he had once occupied that same room, spending many nights in the bed right next to where Terry now lay, his bandaged hands propped up on pillows. Terry had a dazed expression on his swollen face. He was unrecognizable as the person they had shared a meal with just the previous night. Being in that room again was surreal, but Brenda somehow knew what to say and what to offer. It was familiar territory—too familiar. Mike just stood and looked at Terry, unable to offer much in conversation but certainly able to relate.

A few days later, after Terry's extensive surgery, Mike and Brenda made their way back to Riverside Hospital, this time re-entering the ICU where Mike had spent so many days on a respirator. As they approached Terry's curtained-off cubicle, Brenda noticed her favorite ICU nurse, Linda, standing outside the room holding a clipboard. As she turned and recognized Brenda, Linda grabbed her and hugged her tightly, asking how her husband was doing. Having never witnessed Mike standing upright without a bandaged head, she did not recognize that he was standing there. When Brenda turned, pointing to Mike, Linda burst into tears.

"I never get to see something like this!" she cried.

As Linda marveled at Mike's recovery, she was struck by the fact that his friend was now her patient. Terry's expression was childlike and a little uncomprehending as he watched the exchange taking place outside his room. Mike and Brenda entered the room and spoke encouraging words to Terry as he stared at them, occasionally nodding his head as if he might understand. As they were leaving, Brenda placed an envelope in the side table drawer, saying, "Terry, there is money in this card, so please remember to give it to Kathy."

Much later, after the wires were removed from Terry's jaw and he was able to speak again, he said that Mike and Brenda's visit to his room that day was his first memory after his car accident. At first, he was under the impression that years had passed, but then he realized maybe not, since they didn't seem to have aged. He said he felt a great deal of responsibility and pleasure that he was somehow entrusted with an envelope of money to give to Kathy. Terry survived and recovered. Afterward, he began to date everything in his life to *before* and *after* the day he was hit by a dump truck.

Mike and Brenda were members of a committee at their church that coordinated annual marriage retreats, which were usually attended by several hundred people. At each year's retreat, the couples on the committee gave talks and taught classes. It wasn't until about seven months after Mike's injury that they mustered the energy to attend a marriage committee meeting. They did so with the intention of resigning. However, when others on the committee heard the news, they asked them to stick with it. The question bordered on insistence. "If Mike and Brenda are quitting, then I am, too!" one friend announced.

The evening was such an encouragement from old friends who had been there for them in their worst times. In the end, the Palmers chose not to walk away.

25

There are victories of the soul and spirit.
Sometimes even if you lose, you win.
— Elie Wiesel —

On May 26, exactly 366 days after Mike's AVM rupture, Brenda
and Mike hosted a celebration of his recovery at the Bethel Temple
Assembly of God in Hampton, Virginia. As over 200 invited guests arrived
at the church, laughter and chatter swelled to volumes that required people to
bend nearer to each other to hear conversation. There were heaping platters
of food, most of it prepared by friends. The place fell silent when Brenda
and Mike stood up to speak together. It was their first time giving a speech
since Mike's illness. Mike cut a handsome figure in his sports jacket and
black shirt. To everyone in the room, he probably looked far more recovered
than he was, because in the weeks prior, he and Brenda had spent a good
deal of time rehearsing their speech, complete with well-timed wisecracks.
Their old, familiar method of doing a speech—a zippered style of taking
turns—was well-suited to Mike's condition, because it automatically gave
him the prompting he needed. Brenda would say something. Mike would
respond. Then she'd build off what he said. He'd build off what she said. She
typed the whole thing in large print and kept the sentences short, using two
different font colors, one for herself, and the other for him. She put them in
a loose-leaf notebook, and several times a day for weeks, she and Mike sat
together and rehearsed their lines. Each rehearsal took them thirty to forty-
five minutes. By the time the celebration day arrived, the speech was old hat
for both, whittled down to more like twenty minutes because all the "fluff"
had been removed.

"I've been told that the waiting room was kind of crowded while I was unconscious," Mike said. "I guess this is the reason why!" Laughter rolled through the room. He surveyed all the smiling faces in the crowd. "My dad always said that you could tell a lot about a man by how many people show up for his funeral. Brenda says it would have been a BIG one!"

The rest of the speech was an expression of gratitude for the prayers, support, and Mike's still-progressing recovery. Like an Oscar acceptance speech, it was largely a roll call of people they wanted to thank: the friends, family, doctors, nurses, therapists, and even some relative strangers who simply knew Mike's story through prayer circles.

Also in attendance were Spencer's parents. Spencer's mom, Kathie, took the stage after Mike. The room fell quiet as she leaned into the microphone with a smile and began to speak.

"I first met the Palmers one year ago but actually had started praying for them a few days prior," she said. Everyone in the room was rapt. She then shared elaborated about the prayer request she had received before leaving for the Caribbean cruise with her husband, how she double-checked on Mike's name, even though she knew God would know for whom her prayers were intended either way.

"Little did I know then that in a few short days, we would actually meet, and our lives would be forever changed but forever connected."

She detailed how she had received a call from the hospital, how Spencer was shot in the head by a stranger at a party, and how he ended up in the ICU next to Mike.

"I was told he was not expected to make it. I had to remind myself that God was in control of whether Spencer made it or not, and that is where I put my hope."

Kathie had trouble getting off that cruise ship heading toward the Caribbean, so thirty-six hours passed between the phone call and the moment she stood next to her son in his hospital bed. She saw Mike for the first time during that awful 37th hour. She now referred to him as her son's roommate.

"Over the next week, Brenda and I became soul sisters. The ICU waiting room would be full of people talking and laughing and crying and praying and singing, phones ringing, and constant interruptions. I really felt like I was in the middle of a terrible nightmare, and at any minute I would wake up and find out that it all really wasn't true. But it was true, and in the midst of all this craziness, I would glance across the room and see Brenda. Our eyes would meet, and I knew she was feeling exactly what I was feeling—the overwhelming shock of it all, but not without the inexpressible hope that comes only from knowing Jesus. I believe the gift God gave us both at that time was each other. Well, as most of you know, God spared Mike's life and took Spencer home to be with Him."

Mike was always moved to tears by Spencer's story, but this was the first time he had heard it from Kathie. He was overcome with survivor's guilt. Like everyone else in the room, he waited with bated breath to learn how she could stand up at that podium now, smiling, grateful for his relatively happy ending, which stood in such stark contrast to the tragedy in her own life.

"Seeing Mike walk up to my door after only seeing him in the intensive care unit made my heart leap with joy," she explained. *It confirmed to me what I already knew, that my God is an awesome God who is still in the miracle business.*

"The question that some of you may be asking yourself now is, 'How could I possibly have joy?' I lost my child, my only son. 'What is wrong with this woman? Is she in denial?' If God is a God of miracles, why did he heal Mike and not Spencer? The miracle would have been just as great. After all, Spencer was only twenty-one. He was young. He had his entire life ahead of him. Mike was much older, twice his age, and had accomplished so much already. Spencer had a 3-year-old son, who may never remember him. Mike's children are grown and had the privilege of having him throughout their adolescence.

"Spencer tended to live on the edge and didn't have a clue as to what he wanted to be when he grew up. Mike, on the other hand, was a godly man, and very successful in his career. Did God love Mike more

than Spencer? Did God love Brenda more than me? Did the people who prayed for Mike have a better connection to God than those who prayed for Spencer? Is there a measuring stick that God uses to determine who gets to stay and who has to go?

"I do not have the answers as to why Spencer was taken and Mike was left here. In I Peter 3:22 in the Message Bible, *it says that Jesus has the last word on everything and everybody—from angels to armies. He is standing right alongside God, and what He says goes. What I did know for sure at this point was that twenty years ago, I had made the decision to ask Jesus Christ to come into my heart to be my Lord and Savior, and I have never been the same since. Throughout the good times and the bad times, He continues to show me that He will never leave me nor forsake me and that He is worthy of my trust.*

"The Bible says that God's ways are not our ways and that His thoughts are not our thoughts. It also says that He is no respecter of persons. He does not love one of us more than He loves another. However, he has a destiny for all of us to fulfill, and He will not take you home until your purpose on earth is finished.

"But, what about all that hope I had, you may ask. Hope is a very hard thing to explain. It is not pretending that pain and troubles do not exist. All I can tell you is that my hope comes from Jesus Christ being the anchor of my soul. Because of Him, I have an endless hope, not a hopeless end. You see, I believe with all that I am that my son is alive and well today because of Jesus. He might not be where I can see him or I can touch him or I can talk to him, but someday I will. This is just a comma, not a period. The next time I see my son, we will never again be separated. That is hope.

"I have a cute little illustration about hope that I heard one time. There was a little boy who was standing at the foot of an escalator in a department store intently watching the handrail. He never took his eyes off the handrail as the escalator kept going around and round. A salesclerk noticed him and asked him if he was lost. He said, 'Nope, I'm just waiting for my chewing gum to come back.' I thought of Mike when I heard that story. You know, Brenda jokingly says that if Mike weren't so smart, he would have been fully recovered by now. But seriously, if any of you are

in a wringer, in a hopeless situation, be like this little boy, waiting for his chewing gum to come back. Stand firm in your faith. Be patient and trust God. Then get busy with your life. There is work to be done.

"I would like to end with something that has kept running through my mind over the past year—something that I have heard my entire life as I'm sure you have, too. I have always heard that losing a child would be the worst possible thing that could happen to you. As painful as that reality has been in my own life this past year, I can tell you, that is not the worst thing that can happen to you. I believe the worst thing that can happen to you is to have the knowledge that Jesus Christ loves you so much that He died for you and you have chosen to ignore it—to go your own way and not accept Him as Truth.

"I stand before you tonight by the grace of God through Jesus Christ and tell you, because of Him, I can honestly say, 'All is well with my soul.' May our Lord, who does not love you any less than He loves me, give you hope tonight wherever you may need it."

Mike and Brenda speaking at one-year celebration, 5/2001

26

He wants us to know beyond a shadow of a doubt that He is who He says He is and that He does what He says He will do, regardless of the way things look today, and the length of time required in the process.
— Brenda Palmer, 2018 —

Several months after the celebration of Mike's recovery, Amanda traveled to London for a semester abroad. She emailed often, but one email stood out to Brenda, who was out in the yard that day raking leaves. The work was therapy for yet another overwhelming day, a day of wanting to give up and being hard-pressed to think of a reason to keep trying so hard but not even having a clue what giving up would look like. Amanda wrote:

"It's a hard thing to see your parents so sad, especially when they haven't had a sad day as far back as you can remember. It's even harder when you can't share in the same feeling...because, honestly, I don't feel sad in the least bit. I guess I'm not in the heat of it. And I don't see Dad so sad every day. I'm just so happy and thankful to know that both of my parents are waiting for me at home.

"Even if Dad up and quit everything today, I still couldn't be sad about what has happened. He's here. And I wasn't raised to feel sorry for people that have to work hard at things. I was raised to admire people that stick to it and look for a challenge so that I would work my own self to the limits. I don't feel sorry that Dad has to work so hard at what he's doing. I'm amazed that he can do it, and I admire him for doing it, and I can only hope that I would have the same tenacity. I'm more amazed at him now than I was

199

last year. Sure, he can't do things as fast as he used to do...but in the end, does the amount of work that he accomplished matter, or does his character in overcoming and 'rejoicing in his trials' matter? I hope that Dad can regain his futuristic viewpoint and see today for what it is—a test, and one that he's passing brilliantly."

Brenda read and reread the email many times, startled by a message that, in some ways, was germinated from a seed she herself planted years earlier. Isn't it a mother's great wish to see her child put the lessons of childhood into real-life practice as an adult, especially when they're modeled after a wise and loving God? Amanda was holding up a mirror to Brenda, one that she was having trouble finding on her own, and one that she desperately needed. Reflected in its glass, stripped of the heavy layers of all that was lost yesterday and all that might still be missing tomorrow, she saw the naked, pure, and powerful miracle of all that is simply today.

In the fall of 2002, more than two years after Mike suffered his catastrophic AVM rupture, Amanda asked him to build her a coffee table. She didn't want just any coffee table, though. She wanted "the one with ten drawers, just like the one at Restoration Hardware." Was her request a reflection of just how far he'd come? Yes, he could talk, walk, feed himself, deliver rehearsed speeches, fix things, and even laugh, but Mike was still a far cry from his former self. Amanda felt it was time someone raised the bar. She knew she was the only one who could make tall requests of him and expect him to comply. That had been the nature of their relationship her entire life. Mike continually indulged her.

Tasks that went above and beyond daily routine were still challenging for him to do on his own, and he worked at a tortoise pace compared with his former self. Moreover, he was not passionately initiating much of anything, because everything was such a slog and puzzle. He merely responded to requests.

Soon after Amanda asked for her coffee table, Mike announced that he was going out to buy some wood. The problem was, he couldn't remember the name of the lumber company where he purchased wood for projects like this, so he and Brenda prayed on it before he left. GPS and smart phones were not in existence at the time, so Brenda worried he would get lost, but eventually he came back with wood strapped to the top of the Jeep. Brenda pretended that the whole thing was to be expected. She didn't want to know how he did it.

The process of constructing the table was not so simple. It was a long and arduous process. Mike began by gluing lots of strips of wood together.

"What are you doing?" Brenda asked.

"This is what Amanda asked for."

Brenda didn't think so, but the next time they were in the mall, they stopped by Restoration Hardware and she saw for herself that the table did indeed have a butcher-block top. Occasionally, she peeked into the shop to see what was going on, but she couldn't see much progress. She kept praying, and he kept returning to the shop.

Amanda's birthday in March came and went. By then, her boyfriend, Tim, had proposed. Mike decided the table would be an engagement present. Sure enough, he presented it to them eight months later at their engagement party in November 2003. Mike even autographed the underside of one of the drawers.

Of the thirty or forty guests in attendance, including Spencer's parents and little boy, very few in the room grasped the magnitude of this accomplishment. It had taken Mike more than a year to build what normally would have taken him about a month, but the result was a replica of the

Amanda's coffee table made by her dad, 3/2004

store piece. Dr. Raymer, the speech pathologist at Old Dominion, once pointed out that Mike's success in recovery had everything to do with his utter unwillingness to quit and his family's determination to get back as much of him as possible. That table was a three-dimensional tribute to Mike's spirit and to his daughter's raising of the bar.

Yet it represented so much more than a daughter's faith and love for her father. It was a marker of Mike's recovery. Completing Amanda's custom coffee table not only reminded him of some of his woodworking skills but also restored a measure of his confidence. More important, it gave him a shot of ambition. He spent much of the next year remodeling the utility room where Brenda now prominently displays a favorite verse in the window to help keep things in perspective: "Now to Him who is able to do exceedingly abundantly beyond all that we ask or think, according to the power that works within us" (Ephesians 3:20).

The next year, Mike remodeled the bathroom and living room, both in pristine Craftsmen style, something right out of a magazine. There were roadblocks and seemingly insurmountable challenges along the way. Finding a path around them was the business of every single day, but that is what engineers do. They find a way to solve the problem: nail guns can replace hammering. Friends marvel at the transformation of Mike and of the completed projects, a tangible reminder of a creator "who gives life to the dead and calls into being that which does not exist" (Romans 4:17).

During Mike's time in rehab, the lady who cleaned his room randomly announced to Brenda one day: "Your husband is in the potter's shed, but do not doubt that he will return." Brenda recognized the comment as a reference to scripture: "Go down to the potter's house, and there I will give you my message. So I went down to the potter's house, and I saw him working at the wheel. But the pot he was shaping from the clay was marred in his hands; so the potter formed it into another pot, shaping it as seemed best to him." (Jeremiah 18:2-4)

As it turns out, that hospital employee, a modern-day prophet, was glimpsing the future. Over time, Mike did emerge from the potter's shed, the same material—but molded into a new man.

Recently, the Palmers obtained Mike's original medical records and brain scans. Amanda, who started her career as an Exxon engineer but is now an emergency-department physician—a career change largely inspired by her dad's ordeal—cried when she read the records. She was shocked to see the details of the devastation her dad suffered. She saw clear evidence of how unlikely it was that he would live, much less be doing as well as he is now. As she pored over the pages of scribbled but detailed notes, it dawned on her that a patient who presented in Mike's condition would have a 97% chance of death. Of the 3% that would live, only one-third would be functionally independent—that is, without the need of 24-hour supervision, able to feed and dress themselves.

A new owner purchased SkyVenture in 2004, and Mike's involvement with skydiving wind tunnels came to a gradual end. Bill Kitchen's idea, coupled with Mike's design, had laid the foundation for today's booming indoor skydiving industry, which now can be found all over the country and even across the oceans. From toddlers to seniors, from newbies to experienced divers, there seems to be a tunnel experience for everyone. What Mike gained from the SkyVenture experience was not measured in money, and it did not neatly square with the typical questions asked in a job interview, but he was eventually able to leverage his unique background to re-enter the workforce.

As Mike walked down the hall toward the interview,

Morning in 6/2007 Mike interviewed with Jacob's Engineering

he saw a familiar face: the woman who was the head of human resources from his days at Micro Craft. He did not know she was now working in Virginia at the company where he was now interviewing. He later learned that she was only one of many who paved the way for him to be in that interview. Even though Brenda was nervous about Mike's ability to answer questions, the interviews did not cover his work with SkyVenture. Instead, they consisted of a series of yes-or-no questions concerning his previous work in the aircraft industry.

Today, Mike can do most any project he ever could have done. In some ways, perhaps because he has had to focus so much energy into re-mastering skills, those abilities are better than ever. He currently works as a project manager for an engineering firm located at NASA Langley near their home in Poquoson, Virginia.

Mike oversees all manner of tasks, from installation of new equipment to refurbishment of wind-tunnel components. He is often the lead at meetings where the room may be filled with fellow engineers, managers, and NASA personnel. He knows the pressure of communicating highly technical concepts with clarity and precision while feeling like he's in a straitjacket. Mike endures the indignity of sometimes being misunderstood. He may struggle with initiating speech and stutter, stop, and restart when first trying to get a thought out, pausing to route words from his mind to his mouth. Sometimes the words don't make it there, and he simply tries a different method, finding an alternate phrase to express what he wants to say. Even though he "engineers" his way around many roadblocks by taking advantage of technology and assigning others to present as needed, he is often dissatisfied with his performance.

Those who did not know Mike before the injury may initially perceive him to be a thoughtful person who simply chooses his words carefully—which, of course, he is. However, when a conversation involves a detailed explanation or description, it may become apparent to the listener that something is off. When the discussion includes someone working with Mike for the first time, and he thinks he may not have been understood, Mike schedules a personal visit to their office to explain himself, often telling part of this story.

These situations and many more like them are woven into the fabric and reality of Mike's everyday life. He does not take them all in stride, not like some angel armed with the otherworldly grace and patience you might read about in the accounts from near-death survivors. Mike is quite human, and his frustration is often apparent to others. He furrows his brow. He rubs his temples. He sighs in exasperation. Sometimes he's obviously aggravated and may bark a response more than say it. Yet he never gives up and does not accept defeat. Conversely, he also exhibits a patient acceptance of his condition and handles himself with a tremendous amount of quiet dignity. He has no choice about changing his condition but does not wallow in bitterness and sadness. That would be a waste of time and certainly not a "Mike" thing to do.

Brenda is pained by some of the responses to Mike when he's trying to find the words he wants to say. Some people attempt to fill that awkward space by doing things like checking their cell phone, turning to someone else to answer or ask a question, or getting up to clear the table, oblivious to the fact that they are adding a second distraction. Brenda watches him struggle as he tries to think while watching what his "listener" is doing. She represses the urge to ask people to please stop, to just be still and patient for those extra seconds that he needs. She is so proud of the distance he has covered and the way he continues to rise above.

Today, Mike and Brenda lead a full and joyful life. They no longer wake up in the mornings with the sorrow of his brain injury consuming them as it did for so many of the first years. When they go places, Mike is usually in the driver's seat, and as the car swallows the miles of gentle, tree-lined curves around their home—toward the sea, toward Williamsburg, toward the cafés and coffee-houses and gatherings with friends that make their life look familiar as it once was—Mike comments about what he sees. They talk. When they go out for walks, hand in hand, they take turns initiating conversation. He is often the first to ask questions and attempts to jump into group discussions.

Mike enjoys woodworking, even though he still can't hit a nail with a hammer in the traditional way. When the job cannot be done with a nail gun, Mike depends on his workaround: starting with the hammerhead on the nail head, lifting it just millimeters before letting it drop, and then allowing more and more space to fill the arc of his swing with each subsequent bounce and blow.

Brenda doesn't need to coax Mike back into the shop anymore. He goes on his own, often changing into work clothes soon after he arrives home in the evenings. In 2014, he made Brenda a new kitchen, replete with butcher-block counter

Mike in his shop 5/2009, exactly 9 years after brain hemorrhage

tops he handcrafted in his workshop. The room is warm, cozy, inviting, and often full to overflowing with friends who congregate there to share a meal. Brenda imagines God smiling, remembering the words she heard, "I want to see him doing this more than you do."

Stephen has recently put in his first woodworking request, for a new set of benches for his growing family's kitchen table. It seems that Amanda is not the only one who can coax favors from a willing dad, now on the search for just the right kind of wood for the project. The only difference is that Mike now has the help of GPS.

Brenda's love for Mike runs deep as ever, but it is now tempered with the sobriety of knowing he can die when she's least expecting it. Often when they look at one of the faces of their grandchildren, sharing the bond only forged by years together, she silently breathes a prayer of thanks that he survived to enjoy these moments. Yet her hope does not rest in Mike's physical or mental condition. She has stopped trying to fix him. Brenda revels in his good health and his presence in all their lives, but she doesn't need that to make her happy.

"Relying on anything outside of God to be happy will fail," she says. "It's a house of cards and will collapse given the right kind of force working against it."

Mike and Brenda had been in the middle of living their lives with great plans and potential for the future when their nightmare began. Brenda was abruptly thrust into a place where she had no choice but to believe and ask for what she did not have, clinging to anything that gave her hope for a good outcome.

People prayed hundreds of prayers for Mike's healing. Famous preachers prayed for him. Little old ladies prayed for him. Friends, neighbors, relatives, and strangers prayed for him. Yet Mike is not completely healed, not "normal" to his satisfaction. Even so, Brenda says she found faith in a good Father who was always there. With no better offer that she could see, Brenda kept going back to Jesus as her source. Even though each new day brought a myriad of challenges and hurdles, impossible and painful moments that were beyond excruciating, she just kept looking for His face, stopping and asking for the impossible, daring to hope that He could be trusted, continuing to put one foot in front of the other. Frequently she didn't know what to do next, didn't understand why this was happening, and felt like she was one step away from buckling.

Then, lo and behold, she would notice she had what she needed when she needed it, every single time. Gradually, the ground beneath her feet grew solid again. "His mercies are new every morning," as the Book of Lamentations says, and He never left her alone.

"You do know what 'little faith' is, don't you?" the sweet lady with the medicine cart asked. At the time, Brenda did not know. Brenda since has learned faith is a gift. She found faith by experiencing the love of God in good times and bad, again and again. The heavy words from her childhood, "Without faith, it is impossible to please God," no longer claw at Brenda's conscience. She knows faith is resting in what He says, not what she says. As soon as she had a little faith, she had enough faith, because a little faith is still real faith. She has learned to breathe, rest, and lean into something trustworthy and solid.

Brenda stood off to the side and listened as Mike delivered a speech and toast at Stephen and Ana's wedding in December of 2002. He was there— alive and healthy and handsome as ever—bursting with the pride of a father. And then again, in March of 2004, he was able to raise his glass at Amanda's and Tim's wedding, pronouncing blessings for a long and fruitful life.

Listening to his speech, Amanda's face lit up the room. Mike and Brenda have been together and able to joyfully share the moment at the announcement of each new grandchild—first one, then another, then another and then another—something only grandparents can fully appreciate.

As May 25th and the 12th anniversary of Mike's illness approached, so did the due date of Amanda's second child. One morning, as Brenda was contemplating the impending birth, she remembered that the anniversary of Mike's illness was also only a few days away. What were the chances their new granddaughter would be born that day?

That evening, Amanda called to say that she was in labor, and by 9 p.m., Sophia Grace had made her entrance into the world. Her birth gave the whole family something different to celebrate on the anniversary of Mike's AVM rupture, and they do. Mike's brain injury is just a part of their story now, if not the biggest part, and they hope that the telling of it serves as an encouragement and blessing to others who may someday face catastrophe.

After staying home with her firstborn, and while pregnant with her second, Amanda made the decision to change careers from engineering to medicine. Her admission essay detailed how inspired she was by the healers who cared for her dad, from crisis through recovery. She graduated with honors from the University of Wisconsin in Madison, specializing in emergency medicine. After a four-year residency at the University of Cincinnati Hospital, she received a job offer from Riverside Regional Medical Center in the summer of 2017. Today, she provides emergency care in the very place Mike was saved.

In February of 2022, Mike retired from Jacob's Engineering. Mike and Brenda celebrated with a large gathering of friends, family, and co-workers, both past and present at the iFly indoor skydiving wind tunnel in Virginia Beach. The day was filled with celebration and joy, honoring a life well-lived. Mike and Brenda look forward with great anticipation to the future, knowing that more mountains may lie ahead, but believing that the same God who has always sustained them will be with them till the end.

The coffee table Mike built more than two decades ago is as solid as ever, showing the wear of life marching on. It has supported toy-train sets and coffee-social vittles. It has withstood the weight of stacks of college-admission essays and textbooks. It's been climbed and gnawed on by happy toddlers and leaped from by wild preschoolers, the grandchildren of its craftsman. The table is a monument to a family's hope, to a husband and wife's partnership, to a man's resilience, a journey through the darkest wild. Most important, it is a monument to the divine, to God himself, who they learned cannot be bought by prayer or contained by earthly timelines but is always in the workshop, building and shaping and smoothing in increments. He cannot be commanded to move mountains. He *is* the mountain. You can go to the mountain and speak to the mountain, and the mountain *will* answer you back—not with a perfect life, but with a perfect love.

Mike and Brenda

March 2002

July 2007

September 2016

May 2022

Brenda
May 2022

OUTCOMES ARE IN HIS HANDS, but He said to ask and to ask *big*. It has become a way of life for me to ask with abandon, knowing that He allows or gives with knowledge and understanding that He alone possesses. When I pray, I am acknowledging my complete dependence on my Father for all things. When something I consider to be good happens, I know He has provided and allowed that. When something I consider to be bad happens, I can rest assured that He understands and I know I am being held in good hands as I walk through the situation. He has also allowed it and will give me what I need as I need it.

"He wants to see us doing that more than we do."

The Father's responses to our prayers come back to us covered and saturated with His full and complete knowledge, something we simply do not have. Sometimes we get "it" and sometimes we get something else. Even though it may seem like life is arbitrary or resemble Russian roulette, His ways are not our ways. He knows the end, and we don't. He loves us and our loved ones more than we do. He can be trusted from the beginning to the end.

"But at the end, it will speak, and it will not lie."

Mike
May 2022

When I woke in the hospital, I didn't fully realize what had happened. I learned about that over several weeks, which somewhat softened the blow of absorbing fully what had happened. Everybody was treating me differently—my dad, my mother, Brenda, the kids, and all our friends.

At first, I didn't think about SkyVenture and my job. I came to think about those things over time. Designing and building for SkyVenture had been the chance of a lifetime. Working for myself is what I had long wanted to do, ever since I saw my father work for himself. The aerodynamic engineering education was a bonus; I couldn't have asked for a better situation. I was forty-four years old, in the prime of my life, so what happened couldn't have come at a worse time in my professional life. However, as I look back on it, I would not have wanted it to happen when my children were young and still at home. The outcome of Amanda and Stephen's lives was greatly influenced by what happened to me, and I'm glad for that. I see tenacity and goodness and faith in my children.

When Bill Kitchen first approached me about doing a tunnel, I was tasked with making it work and getting it on the market affordably. What it's turned into is a multi-million-dollar industry, a first-class wind tunnel that has even attracted the interest of NASA. Aerodynamically, it's the same as I originally designed it. Mechanically and structurally, it's better. I feel a great sense of satisfaction when I see how well it has turned out. Early in my recovery, my doctors told me that I would see improvement for only a year. I took that news very badly. I couldn't comprehend that it would take a year, let alone not see improvement after a year. It was discouraging to be told such a thing, and I wish they had not said that to me. I think they should have simply told me, "You're going to get better." As it turns out, it has been 22 years of steady improvement, and I know I will continue to improve until I decline because of age.

My ability to speak extemporaneously is not satisfying to me. I am aware of it every day whenever I'm put in a position to converse with anybody. It's especially apparent in meetings or group settings. I feel it limits me in my ability to get my point across. I am completely aware that it holds me back in my ability to move up into more managerial roles in my work.

People often ask me why I don't just write out what I want to say. They don't understand that what is difficult for me to say is equally difficult for me to put down on paper. Just the process of putting together these words for this writing is a challenge for me.

The people I have worked with generally understand. I often need to make technical points, which I find to be easier than storytelling. Occasionally, I encounter a few people who either don't understand or simply don't seem to care, but overall, I feel that I'm treated with respect.

One-on-one conversation is easier for me. The more people that are involved, the greater the difficulty I have "getting a word in edgewise." Fortunately, I have a wife that carries most conversations. We also have many friends who are quite understanding and willing to slow down the flow of the conversation when it's needed.

If my injury had been a physical ailment, I think I could have overcome it, but with a brain injury, I felt unable to do this on my own. The support I got from Brenda and others was fantastic—the doctors, my kids, Stan, Ron, and the church. And I appreciate all the prayers that have been prayed for me. Would I have experienced healing without the prayers? I don't know. I don't understand God's healing, but I think it's real.

I do think it is up to the sovereignty of God to heal. For me it is a process, and I'm not healed a hundred percent. The impact of something like what happened to me is so life-altering that it's difficult to define when you're healed, but you're changed forever. I would encourage someone else who is in a similar situation to pray for healing, with the knowledge that the nature of that healing may not be what you think. It may not be one hundred percent like you were. It's different than that. It's personal to your situation.

I don't understand all the things that have happened to me, but I believe God is in control and that I can trust Him. My faith in God has increased through this experience. I think of Him as more merciful. In the end, I believe God is real and that He is Love.

And I know that He loves me.

Stephen and his dad, 8/2007

The Father and the Man

Poem written by Stephen and read at his dad's retirement party, May 22, 2022

Fathers, brothers, husbands, and friends
Tell me, do you remember?
When did you let your father die?
You say, "This is nonsense.
The man stands here before us!"
Hear me out.
I speak of the father, not of the man.

With admiration and fear, respect and resentment,
The father looms large in the mind of the son.
Always watching, his voice ever present.
A comfort and a curse.

The father, with his hands, shapes earth, wood, and steel.
The father, with determination, solves every problem.
The father, long suffering, weathers every storm.
The father, from poverty, does not abide idle hands.
The father, bold and outspoken, is a leader of men.
The father, whose word is his bond.
Who can be like this man?

It was July, it was hot, we were on a boat.
Three years had passed since the tragic day
When my father's voice was silenced.
Still, there was hope, through struggle and prayer,
That my father would one day be whole.

The boat came to dock,
My father and I at the starboard bow.
A man on the dock, crisp shirt, cigar in mouth,
Voice booming, "Welcome! What is your name?"
A long pause—as my father looks at the man,
Words, slowly forming.
And in helplessness I watched
As disappointment crossed the man's face.
His eyes filled with worry, then contempt.
"Never mind. Have a nice day."
Impatiently, he quickly retreated.

Rage filled me as I watched the man go.
How dare this man disrespect my father!
This man does not know my father,
Who shapes earth, wood, and steel!
Who solves every problem,
Who weathers every storm!
Who does not abide idle hands,
Who is bold and outspoken, a leader of men!
Whose word is his bond.

I turned to my father as he walked away.
Stoic, resigned, distant,
I see a man trapped in his own mind.
The father, no longer watching, his voice is silent.
The curse, broken.
The comfort, lifted.

This is the day I let my father die.
And what remains is just a man, and a son.

And the son looks at the man,
With admiration and respect,

Because in death, there is new life.
As the father inhabits the son.

A son who can shape earth, wood, and steel.
A son who can solve any problem.
A son who can weather any storm.
A son who does not abide idle hands.
A son who is a leader of men.
A son whose word is his bond.

A son who becomes a father.
A father who looms large in the mind of his son.
A comfort, and a curse.

So tell me, do you remember?
When did you let your father die?

Stephen and Mike planning a trip to the British Open, 4/2022

Amanda and her dad, 6/2006

Thank You, Mom

Speech given by Amanda at her dad's retirement party, May 22, 2022

Tenacious, persevering
Loving, selfless
Highly intelligent, open-minded
Driven, resourceful
Resilient and reliable
Inspiring and graceful

An absolute force of nature

To say that my dad impacted my life is an understatement. I became an engineer because I watched him engineer this wind tunnel at home. I became an emergency physician—at the very hospital where his life was saved from his stroke.

I think like him, I laugh like him, I simply adore him. I probably idolize him more than any human should idolize another human. It doesn't take a psychiatry degree to see that every practical choice I've made in my academic and professional life has been about him, for him, and because of him. My love for him informs my love for my vocation and inspires my compassion and empathy for my patients and their families every day.

But this speech is not about him and the opening list of superlatives was not made to describe *him*.

There is a reason that we are here today celebrating a long and accomplished career instead of silently lamenting the tragic early end to a promising career. There is a reason, and this speech is about *her*.

When patients have large brain bleeds, families want to know what their chances of recovery are. Will they walk again? Will they speak again? Will they be them again?

To give some meaningful answer to families, we have researched what those chances are based on what state the patient presents in, how large the bleed is, and where the blood is. My dad presented with decerebrate posturing giving him a Glasgow Coma Scale of 4 out of 15 (3 is the lowest), and a 60-cubic-centimeter bleed with pan-ventricular blood. I did not know it at the time, but I know now that if we had run the calculator on him with those variables, he would have been given a 97% chance of dying. That is just his chance of *dying*. It doesn't even speak to his chances of a meaningful recovery. Which, incidentally, if he survived, was less than 20%.

If you're doing the math, and I know that half of this room full of engineers is doing it right now, that puts him at a 0.6% (less than 1%) chance of having a meaningful recovery from his stroke. Meaningful—in medical speak—does not include working full time as an engineer, by the way. It means being able to communicate and possibly go to the bathroom on your own.

But these well-researched prognostic tools clearly lacked one vital consideration. And that is the presence of my mom.

I only have five minutes, but I could go on for a lifetime describing to you my mother—my other idol. My mom will never have a retirement party because she will never retire from her vocation. So I wanted to hijack my dad's party for just a moment to acknowledge what anyone who knows my dad can attest to. She is the muse and inspiration behind him. She is the engineer and the physician that would not stop until she called back order to the wreckage of my dad's mind. She hunted him down and pulled him back to her and to us.

When we left the hospital, he barely spoke. We rejoiced that he walked through it, was tenuously and often running into walls. His face had no expression.

Now he walks again. Now he talks again. Now he is himself again.

She would admonish me for not pointing out that it is only by God's grace that my dad is where he is today. And I would agree. But Mom, I would also point out that God was very gracious indeed when He brought you to him. It is because of you that we are here celebrating Dad today.

Thank you, Mom.

Brenda and Mike with Amanda at white coat ceremony
entering medical school, 8/2010

Sophia and Amanda, 6/2022. Sophia was born on
the 12th anniversary of Mike's hemorrhage.

Made in the USA
Monee, IL
11 September 2022